CW01111583

UEFA EURO 2024
GERMANY

Copyright © UEFA™

The UEFA and EURO 2024 words, the UEFA EURO 2024 Logo and Mascot and the UEFA European Football Championship Trophy are protected by trademarks and/or copyright of UEFA. All rights reserved.

Published in 2024 by Welbeck
An Imprint of HEADLINE PUBLISHING GROUP

10 9 8 7 6 5 4 3 2 1

Apart from any use permitted under UK copyright law, this publication may only be reproduced, stored, or transmitted, in any form, or by any means, with prior permission in writing of the publishers or, in the case of reprographic production, in accordance with the terms of licences issued by the Copyright Licensing Agency.

Every effort has been made to fulfil requirements with regard to reproducing copyright material. The author and publisher will be glad to rectify any omissions at the earliest opportunity.

Cataloguing in Publication Data is available from the British Library

ISBN 978-1-80279-752-7

Editor: Conor Kilgallon
Design: Russell Knowles and Luke Griffin
Picture research: Paul Langan
Production: Rachel Burgess

This publication is produced under a licence by UEFA but the content of this publication has not been provided by UEFA. UEFA gives no warranty for the accuracy or completeness of the content or information contained in this publication and disclaims all responsibility and all liability to the fullest extent permissible under applicable law for any expenses, losses, damages and costs which may be incurred by any person in relation to such content or information.

Printed in Italy

Headline's policy is to use papers that are natural, renewable and recyclable products and made from wood grown in well-managed forests and other controlled sources. The logging and manufacturing processes are expected to conform to the environmental regulations of the country of origin.

HEADLINE PUBLISHING GROUP
A Hachette UK Company
Carmelite House
50 Victoria Embankment
London EC4Y 0DZ

www.headline.co.uk
www.hachette.co.uk

UEFA EURO 2024 GERMANY

THE OFFICIAL BOOK

Keir Radnedge

CONTENTS

Introduction 6

Chapter 1
Welcome to UEFA EURO 2024 8
UEFA EURO History 10
The Venues 12

Chapter 2
The Route to the Finals 20
Qualifying Stage: Groups A, B, C & D 22
Qualifying Stage: Groups E, F, G & H 24
Qualifying Stage: Groups I & J 26
The Groups: How They Finished 27
EURO 2024 Play-offs 28
The Final Draw 30

Chapter 3
Meet the Teams 34
Group A 36
Germany 38
Scotland 40
Hungary 42
Switzerland 44

Group B 46
Spain 48
Croatia 50
Italy 52
Albania 54

Group C 58
Slovenia 60
Denmark 62
Serbia 64
England 66

Group D 70
Play-off Winner A 72
Netherlands 74
Austria 76
France 78

Group E 82
Belgium 84
Slovakia 86
Romania 88
Play-off Winner B 90

Group F 94
Türkiye 96
Play-off Winner C 98
Portugal 100
Czechia 102

Chapter 4
EURO 2024 Superstars 106
Kevin De Bruyne 108
Gianluigi Donnarumma 109
Christian Eriksen 110
Ilkay Gündoğan 111
Harry Kane 112
Kylian Mbappé 113
Aleksandar Mitrović 116
Luka Modrić 117
Jan Oblak 118
Rodri 119
Cristiano Ronaldo 120
Dominik Szoboszlai 121
Virgil van Dijk 122
Granit Xhaka 123

Magic Moments
1960: Viktor Victorious 18
1968: Glory in Rome 32
1972: Beckenbauer Breakthrough 56
1984: Platini's Record 68
1988: Dutch Delight 80
1996: Gazza Glory 92
2012: Shevchenko in Style 104
2016: Wales' Wonders 114
2021: Defiant Donnarumma 124

UEFA EURO 2024 Progress Chart 126

Picture Credits 128

UEFA
EUROPEAN FOOTBALL
CHAMPIONSHIP

© UEFA 2022

INTRODUCTION

UEFA EURO 2024 promises a spectacular month of international football of the highest quality and all within the bounds of one single nation, Germany. These finals will also be a celebration of the game's rediscovered freedom after the pandemic-imposed restrictions which complicated life for fans, players and teams last time around.

Ten of Europe's finest venues have been approved to host the 17th tournament, and such is the quality of the players from the 24 competing national associations that the competition will attract the attention of fans not only in Europe but all around the world.

Germany will be playing solo host for the second time after an initial pre-reunification tournament in 1988. The Deutscher Fußball-Bund (DFB) also shared in the pan-European staging of EURO 2020. Munich welcomed three group matches and a quarter-final. Back in September 2018 Germany was selected as host for 2024 by the Executive Committee of European football's governing body. The bid from the DFB was described as "comfortably [meeting] overall expectations when it comes to political aspects, social responsibility, sustainability and human rights."

The hosts will kick off proceedings in Munich on 14 June with the tournament reaching a climax in Berlin's Olympiastadion exactly one month later, on 14 July. The format will be the one familiar to all fans: six groups of four teams with the group winners, runners-up and the best four third-placed sides advancing to the knockout round of 16. The quarter-finals, semi-finals and final will be held over the concluding ten days of competition. No third-place play-off is held – this was cancelled after 1980.

ABOVE: *Fussballliebe*, meaning "Love of Football", will be the Official Match Ball of UEFA EURO 2024. It features adidas Connected Ball Technology that will offer unprecedented insight into every movement of the ball and help inform the video assistant refereeing process.

Tradition, the foundation of the narrative for the world's most popular sport, has been evident at every step of the evolution of the EURO. Frenchman Henri Delaunay had the dream of a European championship and also provided much of the momentum which saw the creation of UEFA in the mid-1950s. Hence the magnificent trophy bears his name.

France played host to the inaugural finals in 1960 when the Soviet Union defeated Yugoslavia in the final at the original Parc des Princes in Paris. Initially the finals were contested between four teams, in two semi-finals, a third place play-off and the final. In 1980 UEFA welcomed more countries to the party and doubled the complement to eight teams. Sixteen years later and England, in 1996, was the first host to boast a 16-team tournament. The event's fast-growing popularity prompted an expansion to 24 teams in 2016 in France.

A clamour to share in the drama led UEFA to widen the participation potential for even more of the European football family. EURO 2020 was the first to incorporate the newly founded UEFA Nations League in the qualifying system. This concept was retained in the chase for the 23 finals slots for EURO 2024 alongside Germany, directly seeded as host nation.

The strength in depth of European football down the years is illustrated by the fact that ten different nations have triumphed. Top of the table are Germany and Spain with three successes each; the first and second German victories were as the former West Germany in 1972 and 1980. France and Italy have both won twice – the Azzurri are the reigning champions. They defeated England in a penalty shoot-out after a 1-1 draw in the rescheduled EURO 2020 final staged at Wembley in July 2021.

ABOVE: Italy's players and national coach Roberto Mancini celebrate their UEFA EURO 2020 triumph at Wembley. The penalty shoot-out victory over England in July 2021 secured a second European title for the Azzurri, 53 years after their first.

UEFA EURO 2024 GERMANY

WELCOME TO UEFA EURO 2024

This year's 17th staging of the UEFA EURO will thrill fans in ten cities across the length and breadth of Germany. Since the first edition in 1960, ten teams have lifted the coveted Henri Delaunay Cup and the 2024 finals will unfold in ten of this country's footballing hotbeds: Berlin, Cologne, Dortmund, Frankfurt, Gelsenkirchen, Hamburg, Leipzig, Munich, Stuttgart and Düsseldorf.

UEFA EURO HISTORY

The UEFA European Football Championship kicked off with 17 entrants but rapidly established itself and has become one of the pillars of the international game in the 66 years since Anatoly Ilyin scored the competition's historic first goal on 28 September 1958, in the Soviet Union's 3-1 victory over Hungary.

The launch of the championship was greeted with caution by many national associations. But initial absentees such as England, Italy and West Germany quickly recognised the significance of the originally titled Nations' Cup.

The competition in 1958–60 was organised on the two-leg knockout system popularised in Europe's club competitions. The Soviet Union not only opened the scoring but powered on to the finals. These were held in France, fittingly, with the competition having been the idea of Henri Delaunay, late secretary of the French FA.

Four nations contested the first EURO (European Nations' Cup). France, despite missing injured Raymond Kopa and Just Fontaine, almost made the final – but missed out dramatically. They were leading 4-2 in their semi-final with 15 minutes to play only for Yugoslavia to recover with three goals in four minutes.

The Soviet Union, including legendary goalkeeper Lev Yashin, defeated Czechoslovakia 3-0 to reach the first final at the original Parc des Princes. The referee was England's Arthur Ellis, who also officiated in the inaugural European Cup final there four years earlier. The 1960 final went to extra time before forward Viktor Ponedelnik made history for the USSR.

The 1964 tournament saw the Soviet Union reach the final again, this time in Spain. Hungary and Denmark completed the quartet. Spain had put their faith in a new generation of home-grown youngsters. Their most influential player was playmaker Luis Suárez from newly crowned European club champions Internazionale. Spain beat Hungary after extra time in the semi-finals then dethroned the Soviet Union 2-1 at the Estadio Santiago Bernabéu with goals from Jesús Pereda and Zaragoza forward Marcelino.

The 1968 event saw the qualifying tournament converted into mini-leagues. Knockout quarter-finals were staged on a two-leg basis and the four winners went through to the finals in Italy. Here the Azzurri defeated the Soviet Union on the toss of a coin in the semi-finals before beating Yugoslavia 2-0, with goals from Luigi Riva and Pietro Anastasi, in the one and only replayed final.

The Soviet Union reached their third final out of four in 1972 but were no match for West Germany and Gerd Müller. He scored twice in the final to set up a 3-0 victory. But the Germans' title defence ended in dramatic fashion in 1976 in Yugoslavia. An iconic chipped penalty by Antonín Panenka in a final shoot-out edged Czechoslovakia to a 5-3 victory after a 2-2 draw.

The 1980 event kicked off the evolution in format to an eight-team event. West Germany won that year's tournament in Italy, France were inspired to a first title by nine-goal captain Michel Platini in 1984, followed by the Netherlands in 1988 and surprisingly Denmark – late replacements for suspended Yugoslavia – in 1992.

The tournament in England, in 1996, witnessed the first 16-team finals. Germany won for a third, and so far last, time in dramatic style. They edged the hosts on penalties in the semi-finals then defeated Czech Republic 2-1 on a golden goal in the final.

The golden goal experiment saw a match halted after the first goal in extra time. It proved decisive again four years later when France defeated Italy on a golden goal by David Trezeguet in the 2000 final in Rotterdam. A further refinement in 2004 saw the golden goal replaced by a silver goal allowing a match to run to the next scheduled break. Outsiders Greece took happy advantage. They defeated Czech Republic on a silver goal in the semi-finals before spoiling the party for hosts Portugal 1-0 in Lisbon. Portugal's team included the 19-year-old Cristiano Ronaldo.

There were no more silver or golden goal experiments in 2008, in Austria and Switzerland, where Spain defeated Germany 1-0 in the final. Coach Luis Aragonés's men were only the second team – after France in 1984 – to win all their group matches and knockout rounds at the finals.

Success for goalkeeper-captain Iker Casillas and his team-mates launched Spain's remarkable treble. Vicente del Bosque succeeded Aragonés to lead Spain to victory in the FIFA World Cup in 2010 and the EURO again in Poland and Ukraine in 2012. Goals from David Silva, Jordi Alba, Fernando Torres and Juan Mata saw off Italy 4-0 in the final in Kyiv.

The 2016 finals witnessed both an expansion to 24 teams and France become only the second hosts beaten in the final. Portugal – and Ronaldo – made amends for 2004 by defeating the French 1-0 in extra time at the Stade de France.

No one knew what complications awaited. A celebration of the tournament's 60th anniversary by spreading the 2020 finals across Europe was disrupted by the COVID-19 pandemic. The finals were postponed until 2021 and played in front of restricted attendances in the 11 host cities.

This failed to diminish the drama, which produced four shoot-outs and four other extra-time extensions in the knockout stage. Italy held their nerve for victories on penalties over Spain in the semi-finals then hosts England in the final. "We have done something extraordinary," said goalkeeper Gianluigi Donnarumma after the final – echoing winners down all the European Championship's 61 years.

OPPOSITE: Greek players enjoy their surprise EURO 2004 victory.

RIGHT: Albärt the teddy bear was selected last year as mascot for EURO 2024.

THE VENUES

The ten cities which will welcome fans for UEFA EURO 2024 have long experience in organising football parties, from the 1988 edition of this event to the 1974 and 2006 FIFA World Cups. This year's tournament kicks off in the Munich Football Arena and reaches a climax in Olympiastadion Berlin.

1. BERLIN (OLYMPIASTADION BERLIN)
2. COLOGNE (COLOGNE STADIUM)
3. DORTMUND (BVB STADION DORTMUND)
4. DÜSSELDORF (DÜSSELDORF ARENA)
5. FRANKFURT (FRANKFURT ARENA)
6. GELSENKIRCHEN (ARENA AUFSCHALKE)
7. HAMBURG (VOLKSPARKSTADION HAMBURG)
8. LEIPZIG (LEIPZIG STADIUM)
9. MUNICH (MUNICH FOOTBALL ARENA)
10. STUTTGART (ARENA AUFSCHALKE)

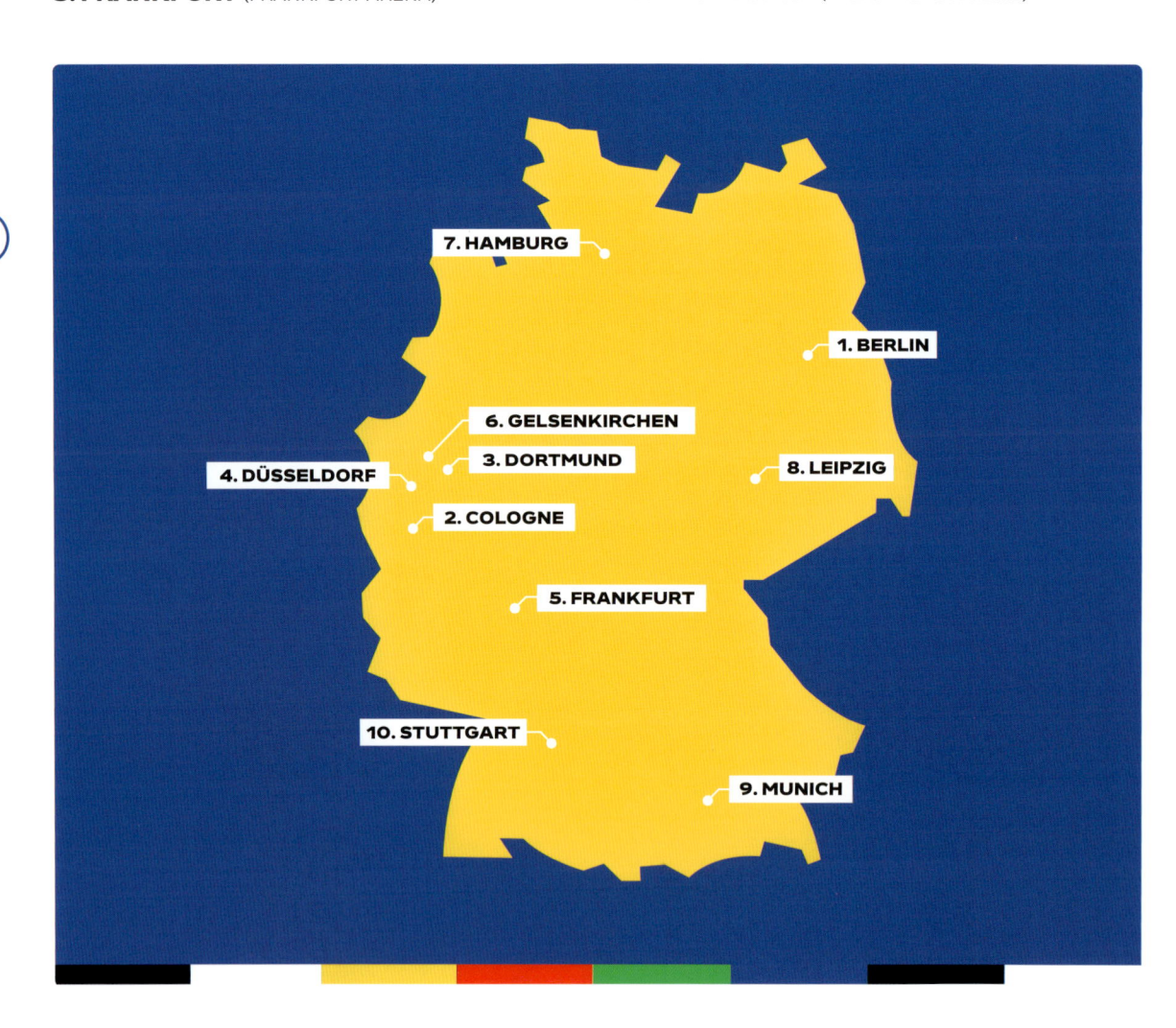

BERLIN
OLYMPIASTADION BERLIN

CAPACITY: 71,000

MATCHES: 15 June: B1 vs B2, 21 June: D1 vs D3, 25 June: D2 vs D3, 29 June: Round of 16, 6 July: Quarter-final & 14 July: Final

The Olympiastadion Berlin, one of the world's most historic sports venues, will stage six matches, including the final. It was built within the surrounding Olympiapark after the city's selection in 1931 by the International Olympic Committee to host the 1936 Games. Local football club Hertha BSC moved into the stadium after the creation of the German Bundesliga in 1963 and 11 years later it staged three matches at the 1974 FIFA World Cup. After major redevelopment in 2004, the World Cup returned in 2006, and the stadium staged the final, one of its six matches. Berlin was also the venue when Barcelona defeated Juventus 3-1 in the UEFA Champions League final in 2015.

COLOGNE
COLOGNE STADIUM

CAPACITY: 43,000

MATCHES: 15 June: A3 vs A4, 19 June: A2 vs A4, 22 June: E1 vs E3, 25 June: C4 vs C1 & 30 June: Round of 16

The Cologne Stadium will stage five matches. The venue is the successor to the Müngersdorfer Stadium, which was the long-time home of Köln. The original Sportpark Müngersdorf was built between 1921 and 1923 and was the largest German sports venue until the Berlin Olympic Stadium was completed in 1936. A new 61,000-capacity venue was opened in 1975, and that arena staged two matches during the 1988 UEFA European Championship. A further new football-specific stadium was then opened in 2004. This welcomed four group matches and one in the round of 16 at the FIFA World Cup two years later. Redevelopment ahead of EURO 2024 has included additional capacity in the upper tier.

DORTMUND
BVB STADION DORTMUND

CAPACITY: 62,000
MATCHES: 15 June: B3 vs B4, 18 June: F1 vs F2, 22 June: F1 vs F3, 25 June: D4 vs D1, 29 June: Round of 16 & 10 July: Semi-final

Dortmund welcomes six matches, including a semi-final. All-seater capacity is 62,000, although the use of safe standing increases attendance beyond 80,000 in domestic competition. The 25,000 capacity South Stand, known as the Gelbe Wand (Yellow Wall) is the largest terrace of its type anywhere in European football. The home of Borussia Dortmund was opened in 1974 when it hosted four matches at the FIFA World Cup and then six when the World Cup returned to Germany in 2006, by which time four corner stands had been added. These matches included the hosts' 2-0 semi-final defeat by Italy, who went on to become world champions.

DÜSSELDORF
DÜSSELDORF ARENA

CAPACITY: 47,000
MATCHES: 17 June: D3 vs D4, 21 June: E2 vs E4, 24 June: B4 vs B1, 1 July: Round of 16 & 6 July: Quarter-final

Düsseldorf will host five matches at EURO 2024. The current stadium, with a retractable roof, was opened in 2005 after demolition of the original Rheinstadion, which had staged five matches at the 1974 FIFA World Cup. Notably, the stadium hosted the second group stage tie in which West Germany beat Sweden 4-2 to put their ultimately successful campaign back on track. In 2020, Düsseldorf staged a quarter-final and semi-final in the pandemic-rescheduled closing stage of the UEFA Europa League. Concerts staged there have featured entertainment superstars such as Madonna, the Rolling Stones and Bruce Springsteen.

FRANKFURT
FRANKFURT ARENA

CAPACITY: 47,000
MATCHES: 17 June: E1 vs E2, 20 June: C2 vs C4, 23 June: A4 vs A1, 26 June: E2 vs E3 & 1 July: Round of 16

The city of Frankfurt is the administrative capital of German football. The current Frankfurt Arena will stage five matches at EURO 2024, further extending the historic status of the venue. The original Waldstadion was opened in 1925 and wholesale redevelopment was undertaken in the 1950s with a German club record 81,000 fans watching home team Eintracht Frankfurt. Another rebuild prepared the stadium for the 1974 FIFA World Cup, and then the 1988 European Championship. The stadium underwent further reconstruction for the 2006 World Cup, and now boasts a retractable roof.

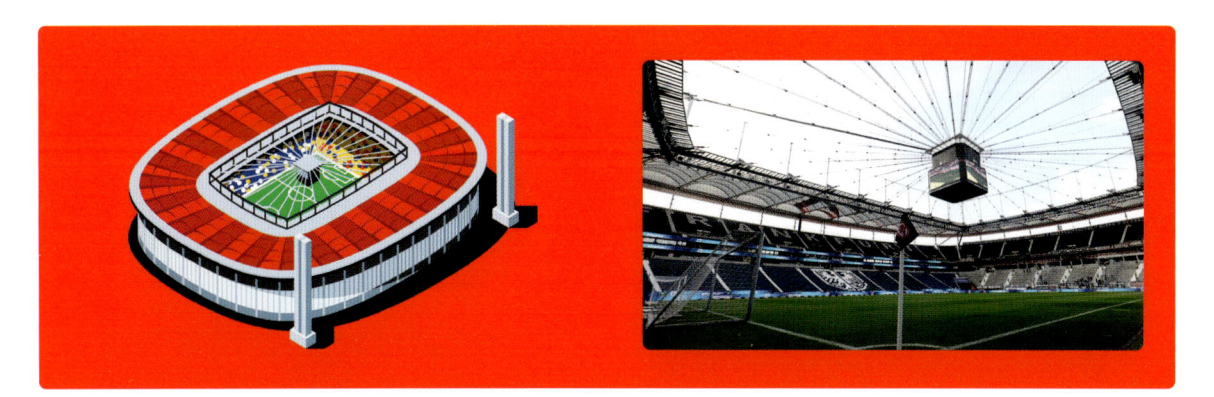

GELSENKIRCHEN
ARENA AUFSCHALKE

CAPACITY: 50,000
MATCHES: 16 June: C3 vs C4, 20 June: B1 vs B3, 26 June: F2 vs F3 & 30 June: Round of 16

The home of Schalke in Gelsenkirchen will host four matches. Completed in August 2001, this multi-functional stadium has a retractable roof, a removable playing surface and can hold 79,612 fans, including safe standing. The Arena AufSchalke is the third major Gelsenkirchen venue after the original, historic Glückauf-kampfbahn and then the Parkstadion (built to stage five matches at the 1974 FIFA World Cup) were redeveloped. In 2004, Porto beat Monaco 3-0 here in the UEFA Champions League final. Two years later the stadium staged five matches at the 2006 World Cup, including the Portugal vs England quarter-final, which Portugal won 3-1 on penalties.

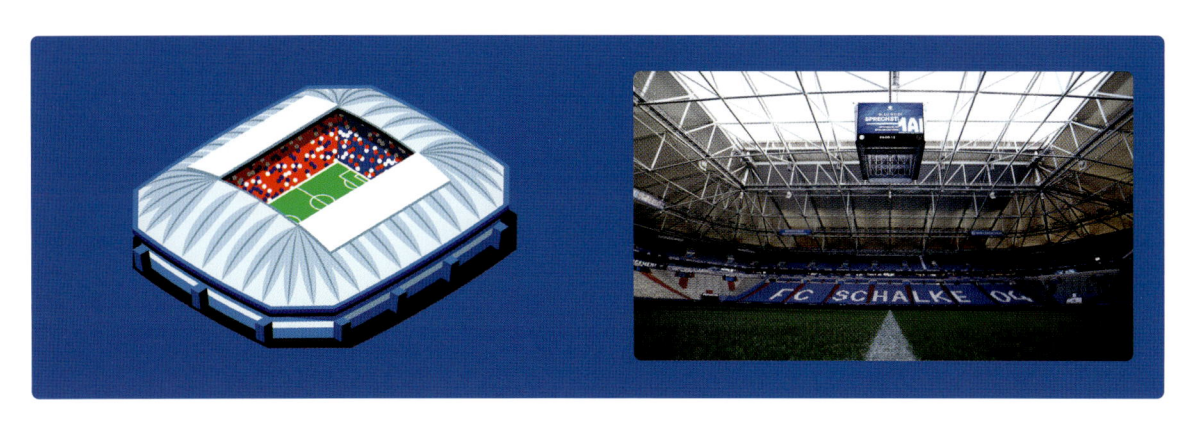

HAMBURG
VOLKSPARKSTADION HAMBURG

CAPACITY: 49,000
MATCHES: 16 June: D1 vs D2, 19 June: B2 vs B4, 22 June: F2 vs F4, 26 June: F4 vs F1 & 5 July: Quarter-final

Volksparkstadion Hamburg is one of Europe's most famous football venues and will host five matches. The original venue, the Altonaer Stadium, was opened in 1925 with a 50,000 capacity. It staged Hamburger SV's German championship victory in 1928. Rebuilding in 1953 lifted the capacity of the new Volksparkstadion to 76,000, the largest capacity in West Germany. Hamburg left their old Rothenbaum home for the Volkparkstadion on the creation of the Bundesliga in 1963. Major redevelopment took place ahead of the 1974 FIFA World Cup, then the 1988 European Championship. Six years later the World Cup returned to Hamburg with five fixtures.

LEIPZIG
LEIPZIG STADIUM

CAPACITY: 40,000
MATCHES: 18 June: F3 vs F4, 21 June: D2 vs D4, 24 June: B2 vs B3 & 2 July: Round of 16

Four matches at EURO 2024 will be staged at the Leipzig Stadium, home since 2010 to the Bundesliga club, RB Leipzig. The current stadium was built to host four games at the 2006 FIFA World Cup and is slotted into the footprint of the former Zentralstadion, which could hold up to 100,000 fans – the East German national team played 48 matches there between 1957 and 1989. In 1998 the city of Leipzig decided to demolish the old stadium and build the new football-specific venue on the site which was opened in 2004. Expansion to the current capacity was undertaken between 2019 and 2021. Work included new access roads and pedestrian footbridges.

MUNICH
MUNICH FOOTBALL ARENA

CAPACITY: 66,000

MATCHES: 14 June: A1 vs A2, 17 June: E3 vs E4, 20 June: C1 vs C3, 25 June: C2 vs C3, 2 July: Round of 16 & 9 July: Semi-final

The home of record German league champions Bayern München will host six matches at EURO 2024. The Munich Football Arena was completed in 2005 ahead of the following year's FIFA World Cup. Previously Bayern had played their home matches in domestic and European competition at the 1974 Olympic Games stadium. The stadium's outer wrap was the first in Europe to boast a colour-switch option. Capacity crowds in Munich saw six matches at the 2006 World Cup finals. Bayern and TSV 1860 Munich were the original joint owners of the stadium before Bayern took over as sole owners in 2006. In 2012 the stadium staged the UEFA Champions League final, in which Bayern lost to Chelsea.

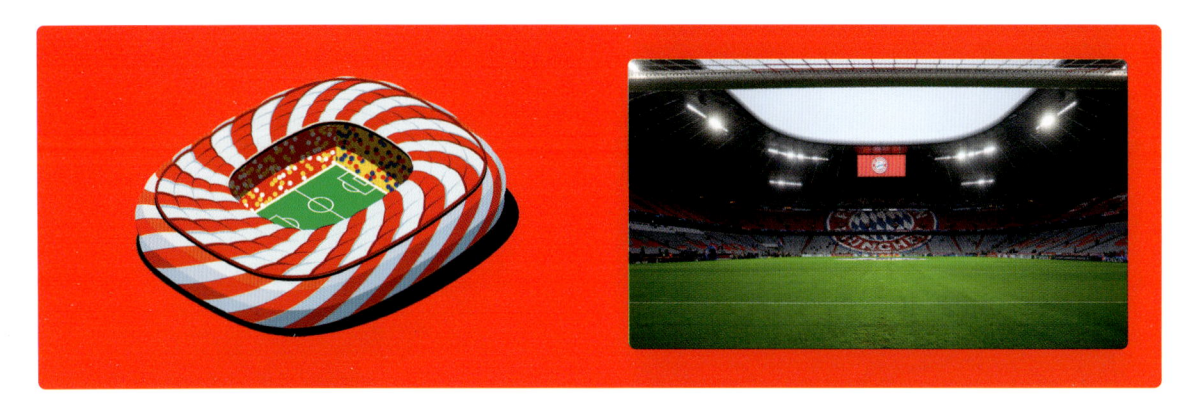

STUTTGART
STUTTGART ARENA

CAPACITY: 51,000

MATCHES: 16 June: C1 vs C2, 19 June: A1 vs A3, 23 June: A2 vs A3, 26 June: E4 vs E1 & 5 July: Quarter-final

Stuttgart will stage five matches at EURO 2024. The stadium's history goes back to 1933, and by 1949 was named Neckarstadion after the local river. Local club VfB Stuttgart have played all their home German league matches in the stadium since becoming founder members of the Bundesliga in 1963. Local rivals Stuttgart Kickers have also shared it for their Bundesliga matches. Stuttgart staged four matches at the 1974 FIFA World Cup and two at the 1988 European Championship, including Italy's 2-0 defeat by Soviet Union in the semi-finals. Eight years later Stuttgart welcomed six matches at the World Cup 2006, including the third-place play-off in which Germany defeated Portugal 3-1.

1960

Magic Moments:
VIKTOR VICTORIOUS

10 JULY 1960 / PARIS

Viktor Ponedelnik lived up to his name in winning style as the Soviet Union triumphed in the inaugural Nations' Cup in France. Ponedelnik was 23 and the star forward of SKA Rostov-on-Don. He scored a hat-trick on his national team debut against Poland in a friendly in May 1960 to secure his place in the team for the European finals. In France, Ponedelnik claimed the USSR's final goal in a 3-0 semi-final defeat of Czechoslovakia in Marseille and then the winner in a 2-1 victory over Yugoslavia in the final in Paris. That game ran into extra time so it was in fact Monday, Moscow time, when Ponedelnik made history. He retired with a tally of 20 goals in 29 international appearances for the Soviet Union and became a noted sports journalist and editor.

RIGHT: Yugoslavian defender Vladimir Durković holds off a challenge from Soviet forward Viktor Ponedelnik in the 1960 final at the Parc des Princes in Paris.

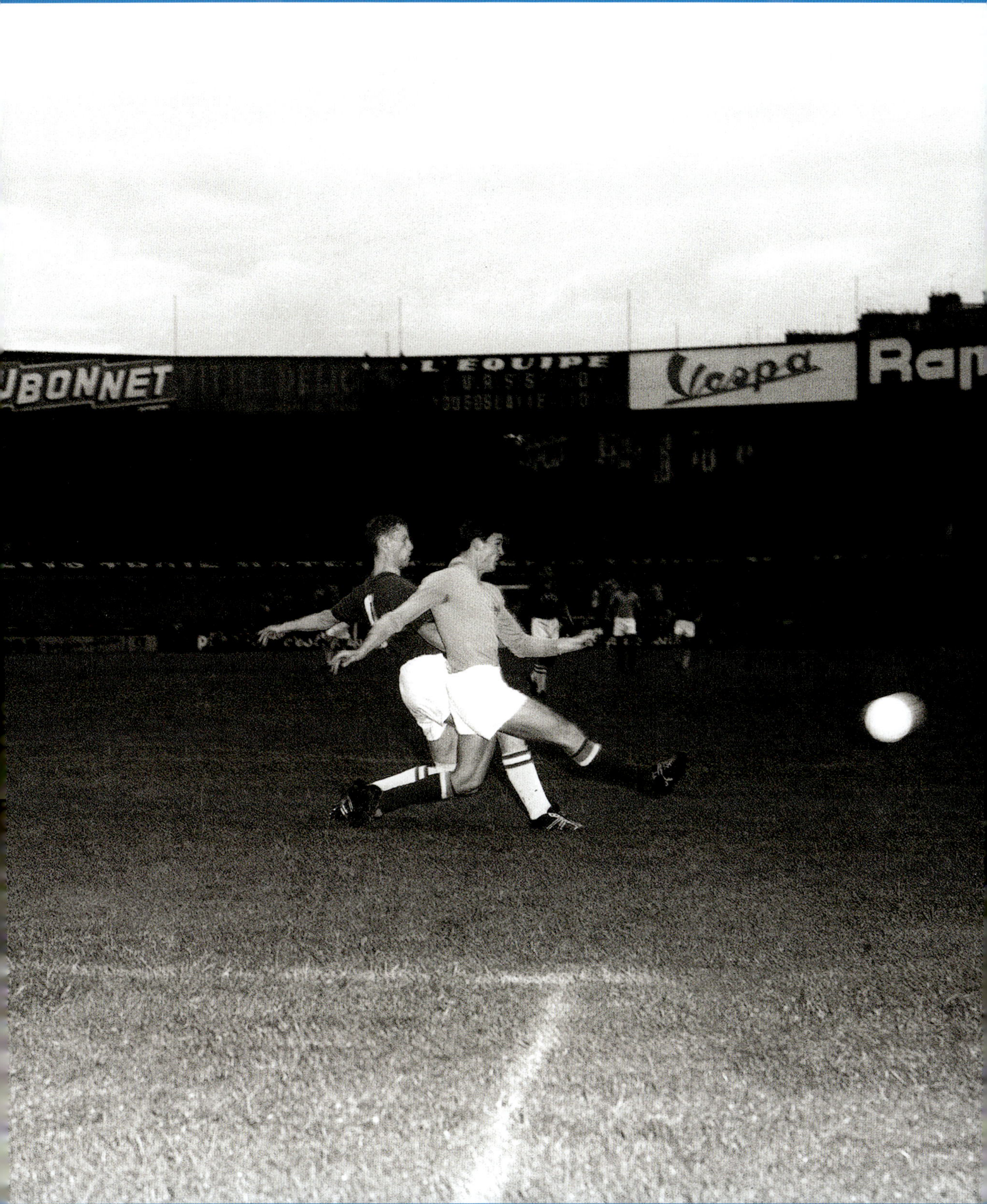
UBONNET
L'EQUIPE
Vespa

THE ROUTE TO THE FINALS

Some 53 eligible national teams from the European football family set out in early 2022 in the UEFA EURO 2024 qualifying competition with dreams of glory. For some nations that meant a crucial first step towards joining seeded hosts Germany in the finals; for others it meant the opportunity to surprise one of the giants of the European game. Surprises, upsets and drama were guaranteed.

QUALIFYING STAGE
GROUPS A, B, C & D

GROUP A

- Cyprus
- Georgia
- Norway
- Scotland
- Spain

RIGHT: Scotland's Scott McTominay was the top marksman in Group A with seven goals.

Spain finished Group A on top of the table with Scotland joining them in Germany as runners-up. Spain lost only once. This was a 2-0 defeat on the second matchday away to Scotland, who owed both goals to Manchester United's Scott McTominay. Manager Steve Clarke's men then won 2-1 in Norway and 2-0 at home to Georgia to end the spring campaign in top spot, with a 100 per cent record from their four matches. The autumn resumption brought a return to goalscoring form from Spain. They won 7-1 in Georgia, with a hat-trick from Álvaro Morata, 6-0 at home to Cyprus then 2-0 at home to Scotland to seize command of the group. Morata and the Athletic Club midfielder Oihan Sancet scored the all-important late goals in Seville. Spain and Scotland both ultimately secured qualification with two games to spare. Spain progressed when a second-half goal from Gavi defeated Norway 1-0 in Oslo. Norway's failure to take a point ensured Scotland, without playing, of a return to the finals for the second successive time. Fourth-placed Georgia qualified for the play-offs via their UEFA Nations League placing. Norway and the prolific Erling Haaland were thus eliminated despite finishing third. McTominay was the group's seven-goal top scorer.

GROUP B

- France
- Gibraltar
- Greece
- Netherlands
- Republic of Ireland

RIGHT: France captain Kylian Mbappé was the nine-goal leading scorer in Group B.

France, fresh from their defeat on penalties by Argentina at the 2022 FIFA World Cup final in Qatar, underlined their continued power and determination by dominating Group B from the start. They won their first seven matches and only dropped points in the 2-2 draw away to Greece on the last matchday. They completed an unbeaten schedule four points ahead of Netherlands with Greece advancing to the play-offs via their Nations League ranking. France coach Didier Deschamps saw his team end up with an impressive goal difference of +26 thanks significantly to a 14-0 defeat of Gibraltar in Nice. This set a record for both France and the competition. They achieved the new mark with a hat-trick from captain Kylian Mbappé plus two goals apiece from Kingsley Coman and Olivier Giroud. Warren Zaire-Emery from Paris Saint-Germain marked his appearance as France's youngest debutant at 17 years, eight months by scoring a goal himself. Netherlands made a slow start with a 4-0 defeat in France then rallied to lose only once more, this time by 2-1 at home to Les Bleus. Mbappé was the group's nine-goal top scorer; five more than Greece's Georgios Masouras.

GROUP C

- 🏴󠁧󠁢󠁥󠁮󠁧󠁿 England
- 🇮🇹 Italy
- 🇲🇹 Malta
- 🇲🇰 North Macedonia
- 🇺🇦 Ukraine

Group C was a testing one, featuring European champions Italy, the England team they had edged on penalties at the final of UEFA EURO 2020 as well as Ukraine. Italy also had bad memories of North Macedonia, who had blocked their path to the finals of the 2022 FIFA World Cup. In the end England led from start to finish, ending up six points clear of Italy. The Azzurri edged into runners-up spot ahead of Ukraine only on their head-to-head record after a dramatic finale. By contrast, England clinched qualification with two matches to spare after beating Italy 3-1 at Wembley. England conceded an early goal to Gianluca Scamacca before recovering with strikes from captain Harry Kane (two) and Marcus Rashford to claim a first win at home against the Azzurri since 1977. This completed the double after England's earlier group success in Italy, itself a first win there since 1961. Kane's second goal was his 24th for England at Wembley, one more than the record previously held by Sir Bobby Charlton. The last round saw Italy qualify thanks to a tense 0-0 draw against Ukraine and a better head-to-head record. Ukraine's consolation was a place in the play-offs.

RIGHT: Harry Kane led England by example with a top-scoring eight goals in Group C.

GROUP D

- 🇦🇲 Armenia
- 🇭🇷 Croatia
- 🇱🇻 Latvia
- 🇹🇷 Türkiye
- 🏴󠁧󠁢󠁷󠁬󠁳󠁿 Wales

A tight and unpredictable campaign unfolded in Group D before Türkiye eventually took top spot ahead of Croatia, who had finished third at the 2022 World Cup. Wales, who have reached EURO 2016 and 2020 as well as at the World Cup in Qatar, lost momentum towards the end of the campaign and had to be satisfied with a slot in the play-offs through their Nations League placing. Türkiye set off in pursuit of a third successive appearance at the finals with a 2-1 win in Armenia but then went down 2-0 at home to Croatia, for whom Mateo Kovačić scored both first-half goals. Türkiye recovered with spring victories over Latvia and Wales and took a decisive step towards Germany with a 1-0 win in Croatia via a goal from Galatasaray's Barış Alper Yılmaz. Wales then maintained their own hopes of direct qualification by ramping up the pressure on Croatia – two goals from the Fulham winger Harry Wilson secured a 2-1 win over Luka Modrić and his men in Cardiff. However, the Welsh then slipped back after concluding their programme with 1-1 draws both away to Armenia and at home to Türkiye. Croatia's Andrej Kramarić, who plays his club football for Germany's TSG Hoffenheim, ended up as the group's four-goal leading marksman.

RIGHT: Andrej Kramarić was Group D top scorer with four of Croatia's 13 goals.

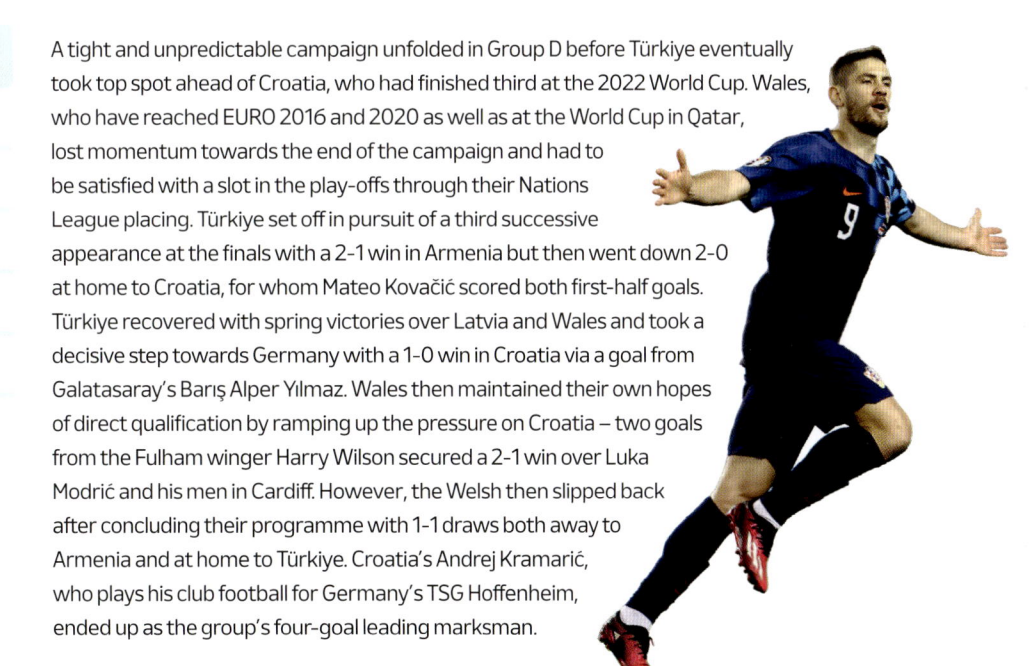

QUALIFYING STAGE
GROUPS E, F, G & H

GROUP E
- 🇦🇱 Albania
- 🇨🇿 Czechia
- 🇫🇴 Faroe Islands
- 🇲🇩 Moldova
- 🇵🇱 Poland

Poland set out as favourites to head the field in Group E. They had reached the round of 16 at the FIFA World Cup in Qatar and were led by the prolific Robert Lewandowski, who had set all manner of goalscoring records in the German Bundesliga and won a string of individual prizes. However, football is a team game and in the end the more consistent performances were delivered by Albania and veteran finalists Czechia. They qualified in first and second places. Poland and Lewandowski had to be satisfied with a further shot at qualification courtesy of the play-offs. Albania had reached the UEFA European Championship finals only once, in 2016, and began disappointingly with a 1-0 defeat in Poland. They then picked up momentum to win four and draw two of their subsequent six games and secure qualification with a 1-1 draw away to Moldova. Albania opened the scoring with a 25th minute penalty converted by Sokol Cikalleshi and conceded an equaliser to Vladyslav Baboglo only in the dying minutes. Coach Sylvinho's men landed top spot with a goalless home draw against the Faroe Islands. Moldova's dreams were shattered in a 3-0 defeat by Czechia, who thus seized runners-up spot. Group top scorer with four goals was Moldova's Ion Nicolaescu.

RIGHT: For once, Poland's Robert Lewandowski was not the top scorer in his group. That honour belonged to Moldova's Ion Nicolaescu with four goals.

GROUP F
- 🇦🇹 Austria
- 🇦🇿 Azerbaijan
- 🇧🇪 Belgium
- 🇪🇪 Estonia
- 🇸🇪 Sweden

Belgium and Austria enjoyed comparatively straightforward runs to the top two places and qualification for the finals in Germany. Sweden, who began with high hopes of qualifying, were eliminated despite finishing in third place. Their final match, away to Belgium, was abandoned at half-time after the tragic shooting of two Sweden fans in a terrorist attack in Brussels. The 1-1 scoreline was ratified by UEFA since the match could not affect the group standings. Belgium were among the first three nations to qualify simultaneously for the finals, along with France and Portugal. A 3-2 win away to Austria sent them to Germany with two matches to spare. Romelu Lukaku, who scored Belgium's winning goal, ended with a total of 14, including four in a concluding 5-0 victory over Azerbaijan. Lukaku's haul was a record for a EURO qualifying campaign, surpassing the 13 of Northern Ireland's David Healy in 2008 and Poland's Robert Lewandowski in 2016. Austria finished one point behind Belgium after coach Ralf Rangnick's men won their last match 2-0 in Estonia. Estonia, despite finishing fifth and bottom of the five-team group, qualified for the play-offs by virtue of their UEFA Nations League placing.

RIGHT: Belgium's Romelu Lukaku was top scorer in both Group F and the entire competition with 14 goals.

GROUP G

- Bulgaria
- Hungary
- Lithuania
- Montenegro
- Serbia

Hungary and Serbia qualified for the finals from a five-team group which was the only one not to send at least one other national team forward into the play-offs. Coach Marco Rossi's Hungary thus qualified for the EURO for the third successive time, while Serbia celebrated a return to the grand European stage for the first time since having reached the quarter-finals as Serbia and Montenegro in 2000. Hungary started on the front foot by winning four of their opening five matches on the way to qualifying unbeaten. The most important victories were the successive 2-1 home-and-away wins against Serbia. Ferencváros forward Barnabás Varga scored in both matches. Serbia had to wait until the last round to clinch qualification with a 2-2 home draw against Bulgaria, while pursuers Montenegro went down 3-1 in Hungary for whom captain Dominik Szoboszlai struck twice. In Belgrade, coach Dragan Stojković's Serbia took the lead against Bulgaria with a Milos Veljković header, then fell 2-1 down before levelling in the 82nd minute with another header from Srđjan Babić. Bulgaria thus finished bottom of the table with Montenegro and Lithuania third and fourth. Serbia's Aleksandar Mitrović was the group's five-goal top scorer.

RIGHT: Aleksandar Mitrović led the Group G scoring chart with five goals for Serbia.

GROUP H

- Denmark
- Finland
- Kazakhstan
- Northern Ireland
- San Marino
- Slovenia

Group H was the most tightly contested of the qualifying competition. Only four points separated the leading four national teams after the closing round of matches. Both the top two positions, between Denmark and Slovenia, as well as third and fourth, between Finland and Kazakhstan, had to be split by head-to-head records and goal difference respectively. Denmark, as semi-finalists at EURO 2020, and regular qualifiers for the major tournaments, were initial favourites, but did not have matters all their own way despite setting out with a 3-1 win over Finland thanks to a hat-trick from new young forward Rasmus Højlund. They lost 3-2 in Kazakhstan, beat Northern Ireland only narrowly 1-0 and were then held 1-1 in Slovenia. Coach Kasper Hjulmand's men then won all their next five matches to secure top spot with a 2-1 home win over Slovenia. Joakim Mæhle and Thomas Delaney scored the all-important goals. Slovenia revived their fortunes to qualify in second place with a 2-1 win over Kazakhstan via goals from Benjamin Šeško (penalty) and Benjamin Verbič. Slovenia's only previous appearance at the European finals was in 2000, while their last showing at a major tournament was the 2010 World Cup. The group's leading marksman was seven-goal Højlund.

RIGHT: Denmark's forward Rasmus Højlund was Group H's leading scorer with seven goals.

QUALIFYING STAGE
GROUPS I & J

GROUP I
- Andorra
- Belarus
- Israel
- Kosovo
- Romania
- Switzerland

RIGHT: Zeki Amdouni, with six goals for Switzerland, was Group I top scorer.

Romania qualified decisively for the finals after concluding the group schedule with an impressive unbeaten record. They quickly established their claims to a place in Germany by forcing a 2-2 draw away to their most dangerous rivals, Switzerland, in the final game of the spring campaign. Switzerland were leading 2-0 in Lucerne with only minutes remaining before Valentin Mihăilă struck twice, including an equaliser two minutes into stoppage time to preserve Romania's unblemished record. The autumn schedule saw Romania secure qualification with a 2-1 win over Israel with two matches to spare. Eran Zahavi gave Israel early hope of direct qualification but Romania hit back through George Pușcaș and Ianis Hagi to reach their first major tournament finals since 2016. Simultaneously Switzerland secured their place in Germany despite being held 1-1 at home by Kosovo. Romania then clinched top spot in the group by winning 1-0 in Bucharest against pursuers Switzerland on the last matchday with a second-half goal from Qatar-based Denis Alibec. Israel qualified for the play-offs through their UEFA Nations League placing. Top scorer in the group with six goals was Switzerland's Zeki Amdouni.

GROUP J
- Bosnia and Herzegovina
- Iceland
- Liechtenstein
- Luxembourg
- Portugal
- Slovakia

RIGHT: Cristiano Ronaldo maintained his record-breaking status with ten goals in Group J.

Liechtenstein were the only one of the six teams in Group J who did not end the campaign with hope of further progress. Portugal and Slovakia qualified directly for UEFA EURO 2024 in Germany by finishing first and second in the table while Luxembourg, Iceland plus Bosnia and Herzegovina all advanced to the play-offs via their respective Nations League placings. Portugal were one of the six teams in the entire qualifying competition to complete their schedule unbeaten and were the only one to win all their matches. They were also leading scorers with 36 goals in their ten outings, thanks significantly to a record 9-0 victory over Luxembourg in Lisbon. Substitute João Félix secured the record with a goal two minutes from time after Gonçalo Inácio, Gonçalo Ramos and Diogo Jota had all scored twice. Ricardo Horta and Bruno Fernandes, with three assists, completed the scoring. Portugal's previous record win was 8-0, which they had achieved three times – twice against Liechtenstein (1994 and 1999) and once against Kuwait in 2003. Cristiano Ronaldo, who missed the match through suspension, still ended up as the group's leading scorer with ten goals. Slovakia, beaten only home and away by Portugal, finished runners-up a comfortable five points clear of Luxembourg.

THE GROUPS: HOW THEY FINISHED

GROUP A

	P	W	D	L	GF	GA	GD	PTS
Spain	8	7	0	1	25	5	+20	21
Scotland	8	5	2	1	17	8	+9	17
Norway	8	3	2	3	14	12	+2	11
Georgia	8	2	2	4	12	18	-6	8
Cyprus	8	0	0	8	3	28	-25	0

Qualified for the finals: **Spain, Scotland** · Entering play-offs via Nations League: **Georgia**

GROUP B

	P	W	D	L	GF	GA	GD	PTS
France	8	7	1	0	29	3	+26	22
Netherlands	8	6	0	2	17	7	+10	18
Greece	8	4	1	3	14	8	+6	13
Rep. Ireland	8	2	0	6	9	10	-1	6
Gibraltar	8	0	0	8	0	41	-41	0

Qualified for the finals: **France, Netherlands** · Entering play-offs via Nations League: **Greece**

GROUP C

	P	W	D	L	GF	GA	GD	PTS
England	8	6	2	0	22	4	+18	20
Italy *	8	4	2	2	16	9	+7	14
Ukraine *	8	4	2	2	11	8	+3	14
N Macedonia	8	2	2	4	10	20	-10	8
Malta	8	0	0	8	2	20	-18	0

*Head-to-head points: **Italy 4, Ukraine 1** · Qualified for the finals: **England, Italy** · Entering play-offs via Nations League: **Ukraine**

GROUP D

	P	W	D	L	GF	GA	GD	PTS
Türkiye	8	5	2	1	14	7	+7	17
Croatia	8	5	1	2	13	4	+9	16
Wales	8	3	3	2	10	10	0	12
Armenia	8	2	2	4	9	11	-2	8
Latvia	8	1	0	7	5	19	-14	3

Qualified for the finals: **Türkiye, Croatia** · Entering play-offs via Nations League: **Wales**

GROUP E

	P	W	D	L	GF	GA	GD	PTS
Albania *	8	4	3	1	12	4	+8	15
Czechia *	8	4	3	1	12	6	+6	15
Poland	8	3	2	3	10	10	0	11
Moldova	8	2	4	2	7	10	-3	10
Faroe Islands	8	0	2	6	2	13	-11	2

*Head-to-head points: **Albania 4, Czechia 1** · Qualified for the finals: **Albania, Czechia** · Entering play-offs via Nations League: **Poland**

GROUP F

	P	W	D	L	GF	GA	GD	PTS
Belgium **	8	6	2	0	22	4	+18	20
Austria	8	6	1	1	17	7	+10	19
Sweden **	8	3	1	4	14	12	+2	10
Azerbaijan	8	2	1	5	7	17	-10	7
Estonia	8	0	1	7	2	22	-20	1

** Belgium v Sweden was abandoned at 1-1 at half-time for security reasons, the score later being confirmed as final · Qualified for the finals: **Belgium, Austria** · Entering play-offs via Nations League: **Estonia**

GROUP G

	P	W	D	L	GF	GA	GD	PTS
Hungary	8	5	3	0	16	7	+9	18
Serbia	8	4	2	2	15	9	+6	14
Montenegro	8	3	2	3	9	11	-2	11
Lithuania	8	1	3	4	8	14	-6	6
Bulgaria	8	0	4	4	7	14	-7	4

Qualified for the finals: **Hungary, Serbia**

GROUP H

	P	W	D	L	GF	GA	GD	PTS
Denmark *	10	7	1	2	19	10	+9	22
Slovenia *	10	7	1	2	20	9	+11	22
Finland **	10	6	0	4	18	10	+8	18
Kazakhstan **	10	6	0	4	16	12	+4	18
N Ireland	10	3	0	7	9	13	-4	9
San Marino	10	0	0	10	3	31	-28	0

*Head-to-head points: **Denmark 4, Slovenia 1** · **Overall group goal difference: **Finland +8, Kazakhstan +4** · Qualified for the finals: **Denmark, Slovenia** · Entering play-offs via Nations League: **Finland, Kazakhstan**

GROUP I

	P	W	D	L	GF	GA	GD	PTS
Romania	10	6	4	0	16	5	+11	22
Switzerland	10	4	5	1	22	11	+11	17
Israel	10	4	3	3	11	11	0	15
Belarus	10	3	3	4	9	14	-5	12
Kosovo	10	2	5	3	10	10	0	11
Andorra	10	0	2	8	3	20	-17	2

Qualified for the finals: **Romania, Switzerland** · Entering play-offs via Nations League: **Israel**

GROUP J

	P	W	D	L	GF	GA	GD	PTS
Portugal	10	10	0	0	36	2	+34	30
Slovakia	10	7	1	2	17	8	+9	22
Luxembourg	10	5	2	3	13	19	-6	17
Iceland	10	3	1	6	17	16	+1	10
Bosnia and H.	10	3	0	7	9	20	-11	9
Liechtenstein	10	0	0	10	1	28	-27	2

Qualified for the finals: **Portugal, Slovakia** · Entering play-offs via Nations League: **Luxembourg, Iceland, Bosnia and Herzegovina**

LEADING SCORERS

14 goals:	Romelu Lukaku (Belgium)
10 goals:	Cristiano Ronaldo (Portugal)
9 goals:	Kylian Mbappé (France)
8 goals:	Harry Kane (England)
7 goals:	Rasmus Højlund (Denmark)
	Scott McTominay (Scotland)
6 goals:	Erling Haaland (Norway)
	Bruno Fernandes (Portugal)
	Zeki Amdouni (Switzerland)
5 goals:	Georgios Masouras (Greece)
	Gerson Rodrigues (Luxembourg)
	Aleksandar Mitrović (Serbia)
	Benjamin Šeško (Slovenia)

EURO 2024 PLAY-OFFS

The increasing importance of the UEFA Nations League, launched in 2017, was underlined by its continued role in helping determine the play-off ties ahead of major tournaments.

Initially the 53 eligible UEFA member associations were divided into ten groups, with seven groups containing five teams and three containing six teams. The qualifying group stage was contested in mini-leagues organised in the 2023 international breaks in March, June, September, October and November.

The 20 group winners and runners-up qualified directly to join hosts Germany at the final tournament. This left three slots to be decided by play-offs in March 2024. Contesting the play-offs were 12 teams who had either won groups within Nations Leagues A, B and C, or the next best-ranked teams who had not qualified directly for the right to be at UEFA EURO 2024.

Some 12 teams were thus entered for the play-offs draw at The House of European Football in Nyon, Switzerland, on 23 November 2023.

The Nations League concept had been proposed initially in 2011 as both a competitively satisfying and financially rewarding use of spare fixture slots in the international calendar. These slots had traditionally been filled by friendly matches which had diminishing appeal.

Europe's nations were ranked according to a computation of notional points per game, known as a coefficient. League A contained the 12 highest-ranked teams followed by Leagues B, C and D. These leagues were subdivided into four groups of three or four teams with promotion and relegation deciding the groups' make-up for the next tournament.

UEFA enhanced the status of the Nations League by incorporating it into the qualifying system for the EURO itself, with places at the finals at stake.

For 2024, it was decided that three play-off paths should each comprise two single-match semi-finals to be followed by a one-off final with the winners proceeding to the EURO in Germany. The semi-final seeding system provided for the best-ranked team to host the lowest-ranked team and the second-ranked team to host the third-ranked team. If fewer than four teams from one league entered the play-offs, the first available slot would be allocated to Estonia as the best-ranked group winner of League D.

A separate draw would decide the identity of the host team for the final. The six semi-finals were scheduled for 21 March and three finals for 26 March.

The Path A play-offs comprised the two League A teams entering the draw (Poland and Wales), the League B runner-up drawn in third position (Finland), and Estonia from League D. The Path A semi-finals were then drawn as follows (with seeding): Poland (1) v Estonia (4), Wales (2) v Finland (3). The final would match Wales or Finland v Poland or Estonia.

The Path B play-offs comprised two League B winners (Israel, and Bosnia and Herzegovina), as well as two out of three League B group runners-up entering the draw: Finland, Ukraine and Iceland. A further draw determined the participation of Iceland and Ukraine and reallocation of Finland. Hence the Path B semi-finals were drawn as follows: Israel (1) v Iceland (4), Bosnia and Herzegovina (2) v Ukraine (3). The final would match Israel or Iceland v Bosnia and Herzegovina or Ukraine.

The Path C semi-finals comprised three League C winners (Georgia, Greece and Kazakhstan), plus a League C group runner-up, Luxembourg. They were drawn as follows: Georgia (1) v Luxembourg (4), Greece (2) v Kazakhstan (3). The final would match Georgia or Luxembourg v Greece or Kazakhstan.

As for the Nations League, the tournaments in 2018–19, in 2020–21 and 2022–23 all concluded with a four-team event hosted in one of the finalist nations. Hosts Portugal defeated Netherlands 1-0 in the final in 2019, France defeated Spain in the final in Italy in 2021 then Spain defeated Croatia 5-4 in a penalty shoot-out after a goalless draw in the 2023 final in the Netherlands.

PATH A

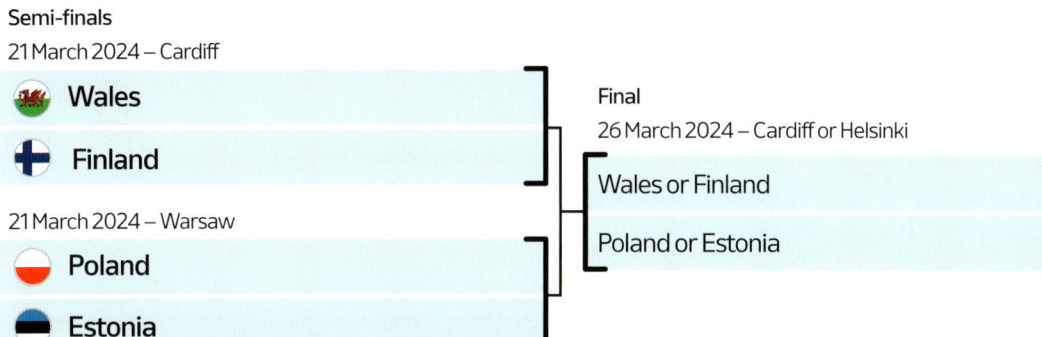

Semi-finals

21 March 2024 – Cardiff
- Wales
- Finland

21 March 2024 – Warsaw
- Poland
- Estonia

Final

26 March 2024 – Cardiff or Helsinki
- Wales or Finland
- Poland or Estonia

PATH B

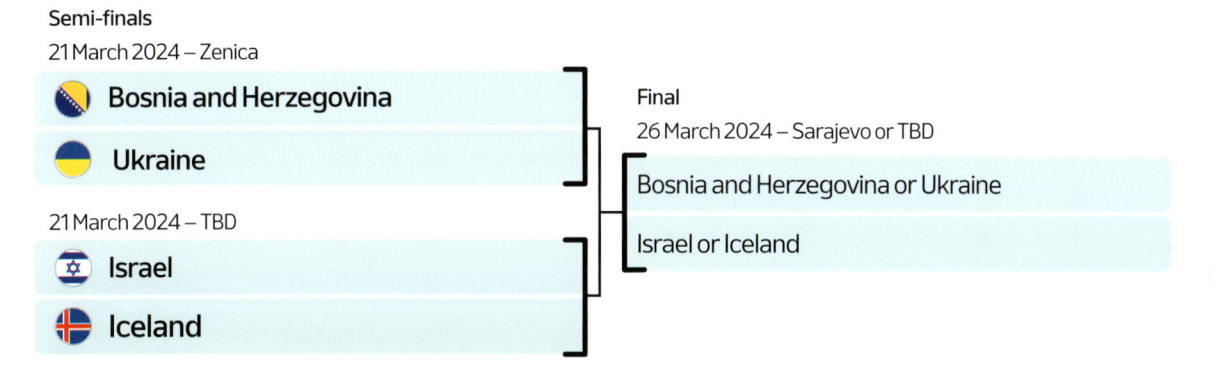

Semi-finals

21 March 2024 – Zenica
- Bosnia and Herzegovina
- Ukraine

21 March 2024 – TBD
- Israel
- Iceland

Final

26 March 2024 – Sarajevo or TBD
- Bosnia and Herzegovina or Ukraine
- Israel or Iceland

PATH C

Semi-finals

21 March 2024 – Tbilisi
- Georgia
- Luxembourg

21 March 2024 – Athens
- Greece
- Kazakhstan

Final

26 March 2024 – Tbilisi or Luxembourg City
- Georgia or Luxembourg
- Greece or Kazakhstan

A modification for the next edition of the Nations League, starting in September 2024, will introduce a knockout round as a bridge between the end of the group phase and the finals. A UEFA statement said the change had followed an extensive consultation process with the national associations but would not add any fresh dates to the international calendar.

UEFA president Aleksander Čeferin said: "The introduction of the UEFA Nations League was a success story, replacing friendly games with more competitive matches. By introducing the new knockout phase, teams will be given even more opportunities to progress while keeping the same number of games within the international match calendar."

THE FINAL DRAW

Saturday, 2 December 2023, was the date on which the managers and players of the finalists at UEFA EURO 2024 learned which fixtures awaited them. The finals draw, staged in the Elbphilharmonie concert hall in Hamburg, kicked off a new adventure for all the competing nations.

An event hosted by Pedro Pinto and Esther Sedlaczek opened with a prelude by the tenor Jonas Kaufmann and leading violinist David Garrett as well as Germany's National Youth Orchestra, National Jazz Orchestra and National Youth Choir. Then a team of heroes from past European title-winning nations delivered the main course of the draw itself.

Germany, as hosts, led the top seeds to their slots across the six groups from which the top two nations plus the four best third-placed teams will progress into the knockout stage.

The hosts open the finals against Scotland with Hungary and Switzerland completing Group A. National coach Julian Nagelsmann attended the draw only three months after being appointed in succession to Hansi Flick. Germany hope to make amends for early exits at their last three major tournaments.

Nagelsmann said: "It's no group of death but a very strong group and we are looking forward to it. We have a very good opening match against Scotland with emotional crowds, in a positive way." Scotland have fallen at the group stage in all of their 11 appearances at a major tournament. Manager Steve Clarke said: "It was always going to be exciting. It's a good group, evenly balanced."

The draw for Group B matched three-times winners Spain with reigning champions Italy. Their competitive rivalry stretches back to the 1934 FIFA World Cup, when hosts Italy narrowly defeated Spain in a quarter-final replay. The tie will be a repeat of the final at EURO 2012. On that occasion Spain won 4-0 in Kyiv. Azzurri coach Luciano Spalletti said: "This is surely the most difficult group but we know what our goal is: to pass the group stage."

An eastern Europe duo, Croatia and Albania, complete Group B. Croatia were third at the 2022 FIFA World Cup last year. Coach Zlatko Dalić had no doubt about the challenge ahead, echoing the words of Spalletti.

England, newly-risen to third in the FIFA World Ranking, were the top seeds in Group C. Manager Gareth Southgate's beaten finalists from EURO 2020 were drawn to open against Serbia. Their next opposition will come from a Denmark side who pushed England to extra time in the EURO 2020 semi-finals. Slovenia make up the group.

Southgate said: "You know the objective is always to get out of the group. We know the expectations, we are getting used to these big games. We hope to give our supporters some brilliant nights."

Group D provides a rematch between France and Netherlands, who finished first and second in the same qualifying group. France, runners-up at the World Cup in

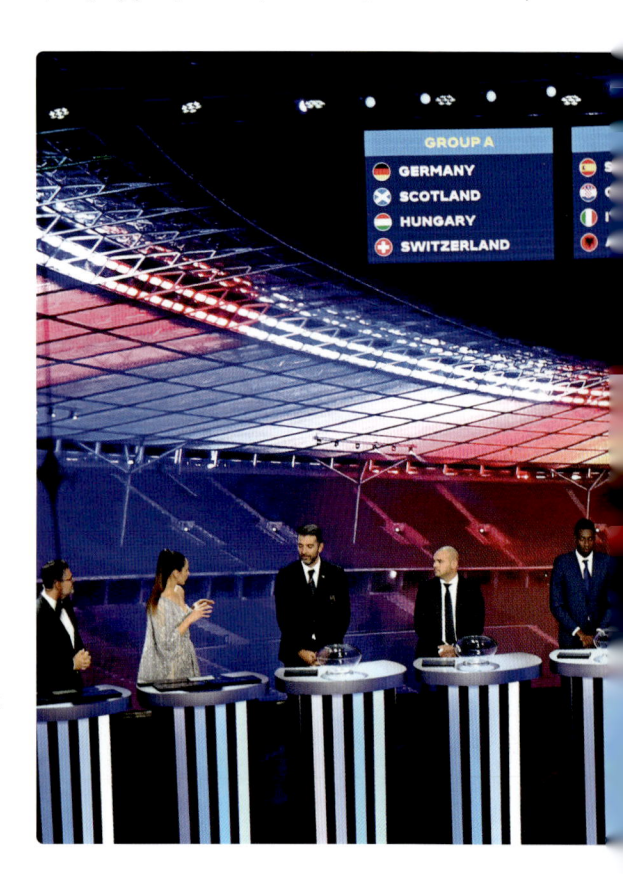

Qatar in December 2022, won 4-0 at home and 2-1 away.

Netherlands manager Ronald Koeman said: "It's difficult for everybody. I did not prefer France, maybe France did not prefer Holland because we play often. Anyway we need to accept it. Our objective is to win the tournament."

Austria, managed by the German coach Ralf Rangnick, were drawn to complete the group along with the winners of play-off Path A (Poland, Wales, Finland or Estonia).

Belgium were the top seeds in Group E. Both they and Romania completed their qualification schedules undefeated. Belgium captain Romelu Lukaku had been the leading scorer in the qualifying tournament with 14 goals. Challenging them will be Slovakia, who qualified as a group runner-up, plus the play-off Path B winners (Israel, Iceland, Bosnia and Herzegovina or Ukraine).

The remaining play-off winners, from Path C (Georgia, Greece, Kazakhstan or Luxembourg), were placed in Group F with Türkiye, Czechia and Portugal, the 2016 champions. Portugal stormed through their qualifying group by winning all ten matches with 36 goals scored and only two conceded. Cristiano Ronaldo scored ten of those goals.

The official song of the tournament has been created by Italian DJ group Meduza, American pop-rock giants OneRepublic and German pop icon Kim Petras.

Prize money on offer to the 24 finalists totals €331m. The distribution system, matching that of EURO 2020, was approved by the UEFA Executive Committee, on the eve of the draw. All the 24 finalists will benefit from a participation fee of €9.25m plus match bonuses of €1m for a win and €500,000 for a draw.

Qualification for the round of 16 will be worth €1.5m, qualification for the quarter-finals €2.5m and qualification for the semi-finals €4m. The runners-up will receive an additional €5m with the eventual champions being rewarded with an extra €8m. Hence the maximum sum possible for the champions, if they win all three of their group matches, is €28.25m.

The ultimate glory of raising the Henri Delaunay Cup is beyond price.

BELOW: Giorgio Marchetti, the deputy general secretary of UEFA, oversees a team of all talents undertaking the draw for the finals.

1968

Magic Moments:

GLORY IN ROME

10 JUNE 1968 / ROME

Italy are the only team to have won the European crown with the help of both a toss of a coin and also a replay in the days long before penalty shoot-outs. Italy had been chosen to host the 1968 finals but found it difficult to capitalise on any perceived home advantage. In the semi-finals they drew 0-0 after extra time with the Soviet Union in Naples and reached the final only because captain Giacinto Facchetti called correctly on the toss of a coin. The final, in Rome, saw Italy held again after extra time, this time by Yugoslavia. The rules permitted a replay, in which Italy's attack proved decisive. Goals from Luigi Riva and Pietro Anastasi in the first half-hour delivered a 2-0 victory. Riva, with 35 goals, remains Italy's all-time top scorer.

RIGHT: Italy's captain Giacinto Facchetti parades the Henri Delaunay Cup after the hosts' 2-0 victory over Yugoslavia in a replay at Rome's Stadio Olimpico.

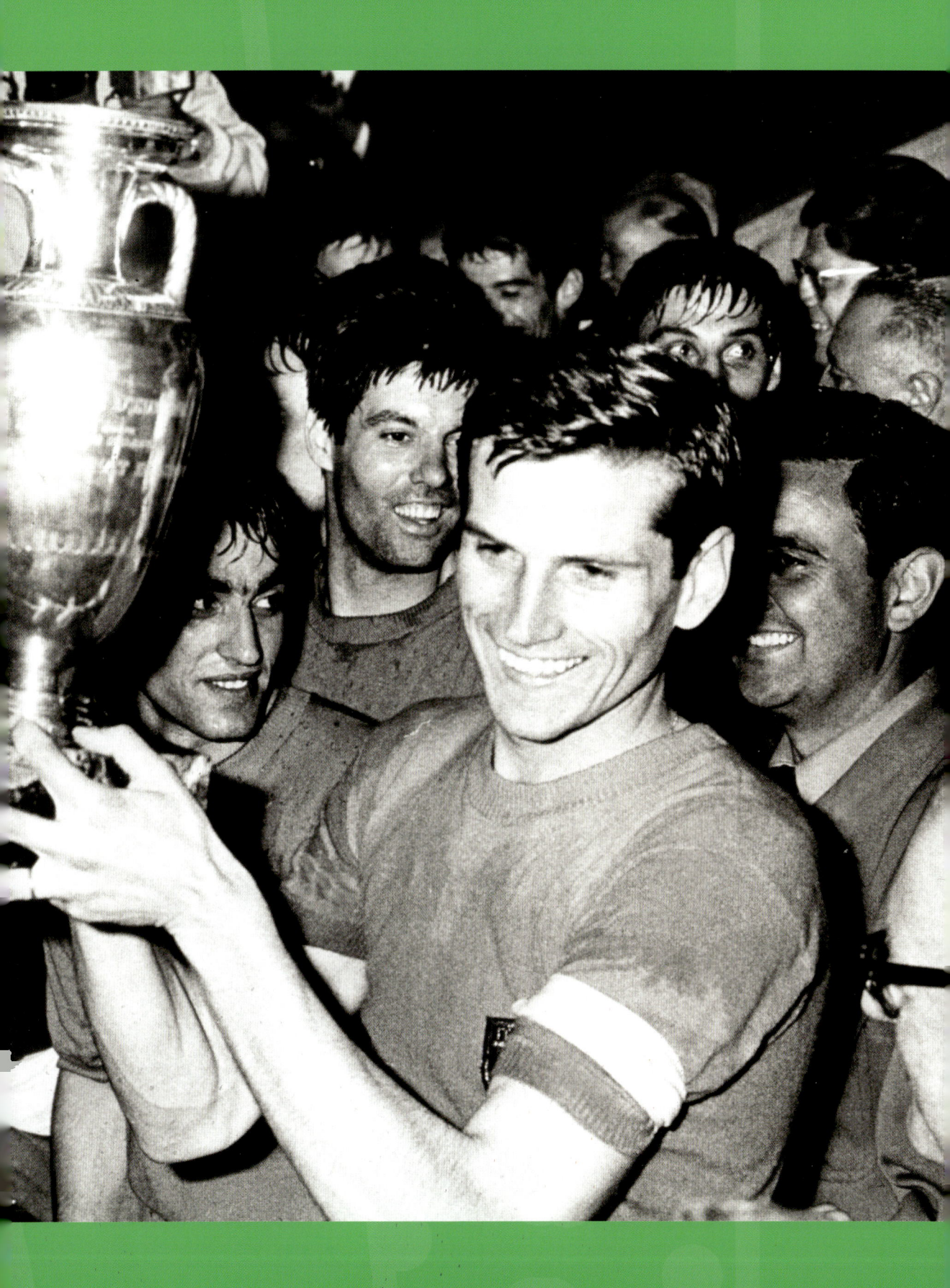

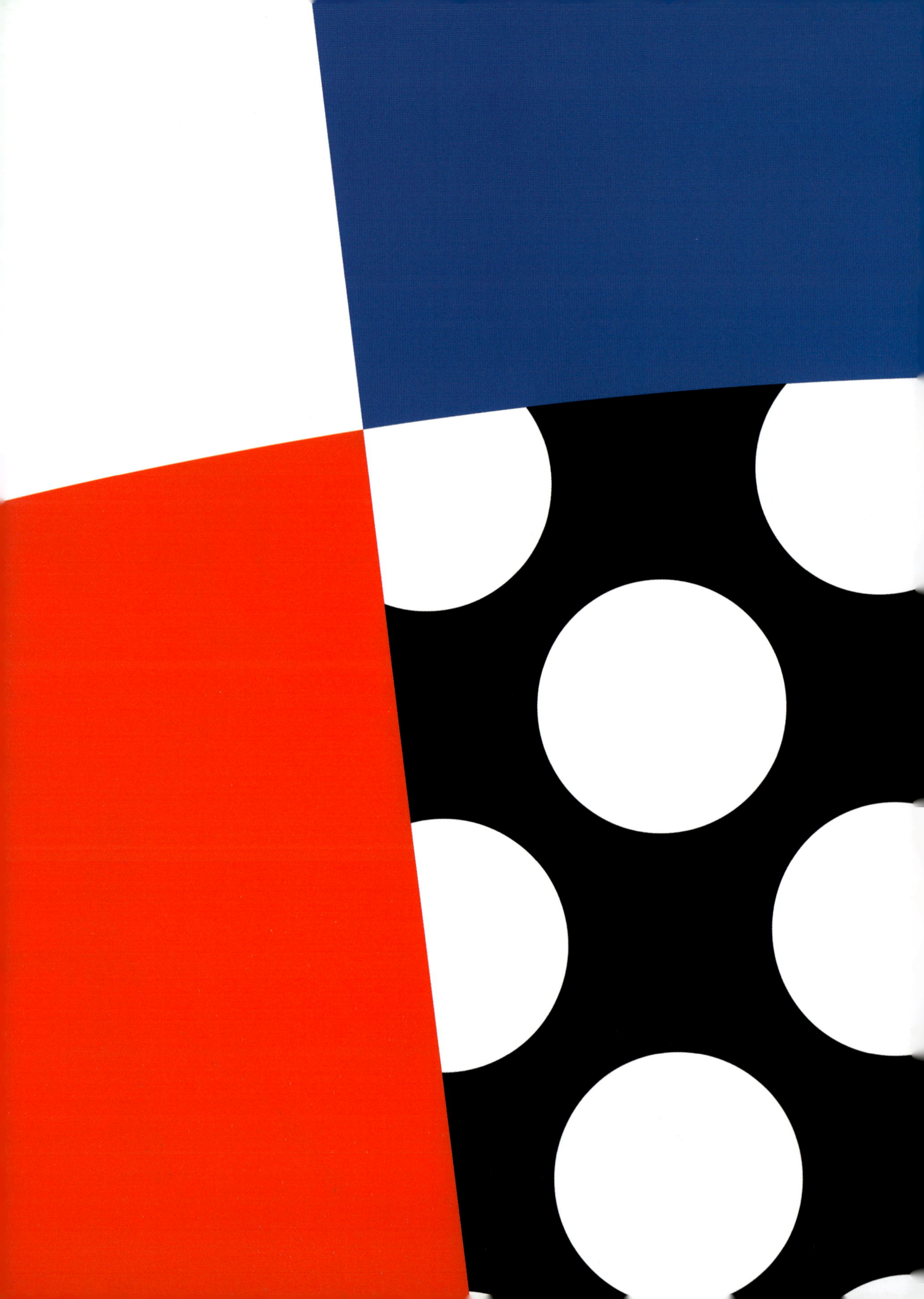

MEET THE TEAMS

The 24 finalists at UEFA EURO 2024 will include nine past champions in Czechia (as Czechoslovakia), Denmark, France, Germany, Greece, Italy, Netherlands, Portugal and Spain. Portugal were the only team who registered a 100 per cent record in qualifying by winning all ten of their group matches. Five other nations completed their fixtures undefeated: Belgium, England, France, Hungary and Romania. Germany plays sole host for the first time since reunification after West Germany's staging of the tournament in 1988.

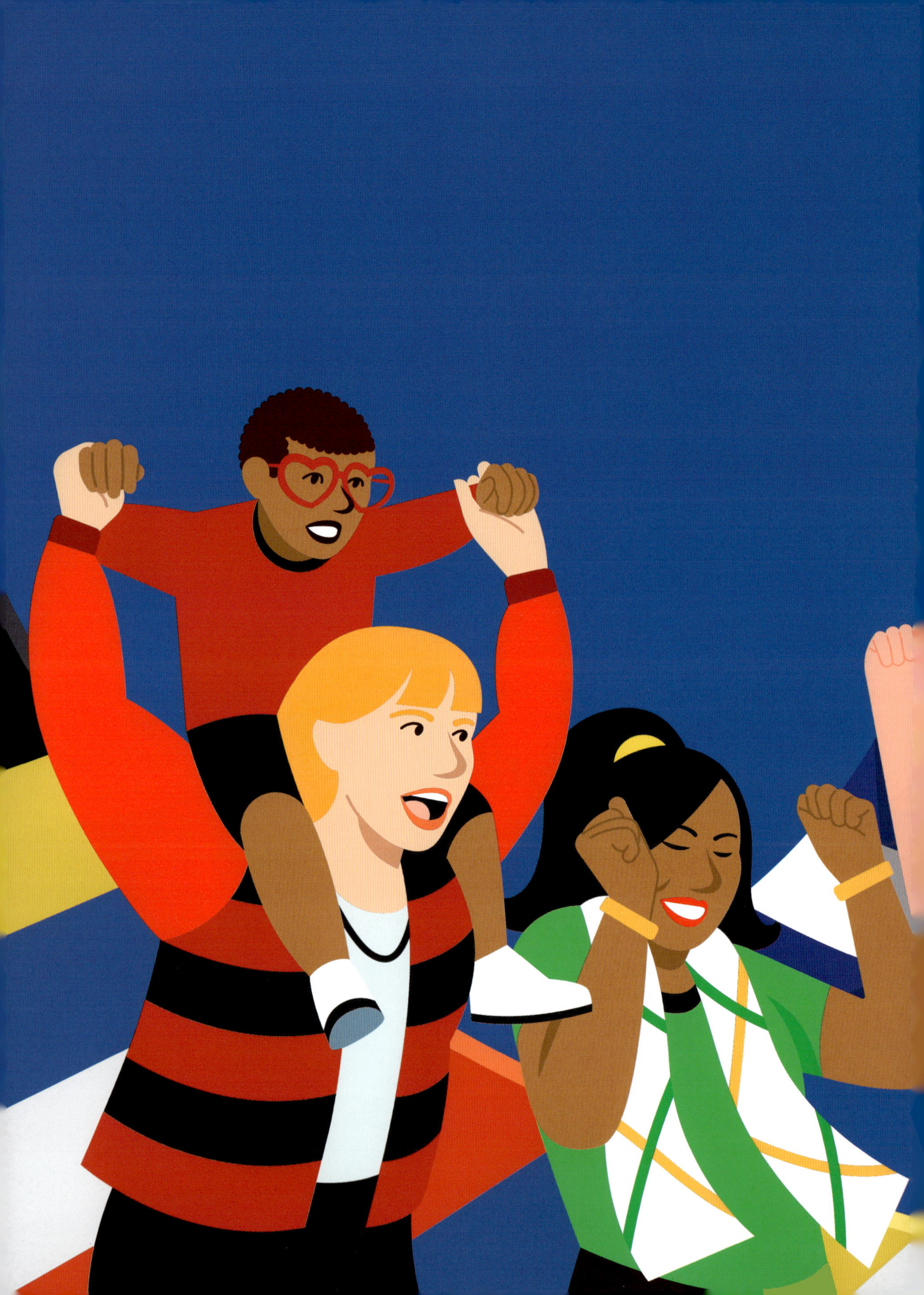

UEFA EURO 2024 GERMANY

GROUP A

Hosts Germany have won the UEFA EURO crown on three occasions, the last in 1996. They have also been runners-up on three occasions. Hungary were semi-finalists in 1964 and 1972. Switzerland were quarter-finalists at EURO 2020. Scotland have never been past the group stage. All four were present at EURO 2020.

- Germany
- Scotland
- Hungary
- Switzerland

GROUP A
GERMANY

Germany prepare to welcome the cream of European football under heavy pressure of expectation. They are seeking to reclaim the winning mentality traditionally associated with a team who have won the EURO on a record-equalling three occasions, as well as four FIFA World Cups.

The German Football Association (DFB) was awarded host rights to the finals in September 2018, just two months after *Die Mannschaft* had lost their FIFA World Cup crown in Russia. Their group stage exit appeared a mere blip on the dial. But recovering balance and a winning style proved difficult.

National coach Joachim Löw brought Germany safely through to the pandemic-delayed UEFA EURO 2020, but pursuit of a first European title since 1996 was halted by a 2-0 defeat at the hands of England at Wembley in the round of 16. That was Löw's last match in charge, since the DFB had already decided to bring in Hansi Flick.

The former midfielder took on the task after a remarkable 18 months in charge at Bayern München during which they won seven trophies – the Bundesliga twice, German Cup and Supercup, UEFA Champions League and Super Cup, plus FIFA Club World Cup.

Flick had worked previously on the national team coaching staff and duly led Germany to the 2022 World Cup finals in Qatar. However, another group stage exit and disappointing results in subsequent friendly matches led to his replacement by Julian Nagelsmann last September.

Nagelsmann, on his appointment, referenced the wave of happy excitement throughout Germany during

ABOVE: Germany, as hosts, are appearing in the finals for a record-extending 14th time. Their 53 matches include 27 wins, 13 draws and 13 defeats.

GERMANY at the UEFA European Championship

1960	Did not enter
1964	Did not enter
1968**	Did not qualify
1972**	WINNERS
1976**	Runners-up
1980**	WINNERS
1984**	Group stage
1988**	Semi-finals
1992	Runners-up
1996	WINNERS
2000	Group stage
2004	Group stage
2008	Runners-up
2012	Semi-finals
2016	Semi-finals
2020*	Round of 16

*2020 finals were played in 2021
**As West Germany

COACH

JULIAN NAGELSMANN

Julian Nagelsmann, 36, became the youngest national coach in Germany's history on succeeding Hansi Flick last September. Nagelsmann had turned to coaching after serious injury ended his playing career in 2007. He was a youth coach with TSV 1860 Munich before taking on a similar role at Hoffenheim and graduating to head coach in 2015. He lifted them into the UEFA Champions League, taking RB Leipzig to the semi-finals before joining Bayern München. Nagelsmann also replaced Flick at Bayern, leading the club to their tenth successive Bundesliga title before parting company in March 2023.

KEY PLAYER

JOSHUA KIMMICH

POSITION: Midfield
CLUB: FC Bayern München (GERMANY)
AGE: 29
BORN: 8 February 1995, Rottwell
INTERNATIONAL DEBUT: 21 June 2016 vs N Ireland
CAPS: 82 • **GOALS**: 6

Joshua Kimmich emerged as one of the most outstandingly versatile right-backs or defensive midfielders in European football after establishing himself at Bayern München, initially under Pep Guardiola. Kimmich, as a teenager, came through the youth sections of VfB Stuttgart before proving himself at RB Leipzig during the club's progression out of the lower divisions. He joined Bayern in 2015 and has since helped them win 20 major national and international trophies, including the UEFA Champions League in 2020. He graduated into the national squad on the eve of UEFA EURO 2016 when he was named in the Team of the Tournament. He has been a regular first-choice ever since, including Germany's FIFA Confederations Cup win in 2017.

its hosting of the World Cup in 2006. He said: "We want to inspire the nation with the whole team [playing] good football. The ideal for us is a *Sommermärchen* [summer fairy tale] 2.0."

Germany, as hosts of EURO 2024, were exempt from qualifying so Nagelsmann had a slew of friendlies in which to build. He made a winning start with a 3-1 win over the United States in East Hartford, Connecticut, with goals from İlkay Gündoğan, Niclas Füllkrug and Jamal Musiala.

The nucleus of Nagelsmann's squad showed few variations from the choices made by Flick. Marc-André ter Stegen had long been the goalkeeping back-up to injured Manuel Neuer while Antonio Rüdiger, Matts Hummels and Niklas Süle provided defensive knowhow.

Joshua Kimmich and Leon Goretzka were familiar partners in midfield in support of their outstanding club-mate Musiala. The latter had switched allegiance to his birth nation in 2021 after playing for England at youth and Under-21 levels.

Other Bayern stars familiar to Nagelsmann, their former coach, were Leroy Sané and Thomas Müller while captain Gündoğan had underlined his qualities in Manchester City's treble-winning 2022/23 season. Additional class was available in Kai Havertz, a Champions League trophy-winner for Chelsea before his transfer to Arsenal.

All this experience and ability fuel German hopes to extend their record of three titles in a tournament to which they were late starters.

West Germany did not enter the 1960 and 1964 championships and were eliminated in the first round of 1968 qualifying. Everything changed in the 1970s. Bayern won a hat-trick of European Cups and provided the nucleus of the national side who won the EURO in 1972, the World Cup in 1974 and, after finishing runners-up in 1976, the European title again in 1980 and 1996.

This was Germany's last senior title for 18 years before a dramatic World Cup victory over Argentina in 2014 in Brazil. The tenth anniversary of that triumph would be an appropriate occasion for Germany to regain their old winning magic.

DID YOU KNOW?

Germany did not have a national league until the Bundesliga was launched in 1963. Until then the title was decided by a play-off tournament between champions of the regional leagues.

GROUP A
SCOTLAND

Scotland learned they had qualified for the finals without even playing. Other results in their group provided the luxury of celebrating without undergoing the usual matchday tension. Steve Clarke's team were finalists for the second successive time.

Back on 30 November 1872 Scotland had contested the first-ever international match when they drew 0-0 with England in Partick, Glasgow. Scots sent the first professionals south across the border into England and devised the passing style which influenced the development of the game across the continent.

Scotland went to the FIFA World Cup finals in 1954 and 1958 while 'Old Firm' rivals Celtic and Rangers played powerful roles in the early years of European club competitions. Celtic, in 1967, were the first British club to win the European Champion Clubs' Cup while Rangers won the UEFA Cup Winners' Cup in 1972.

The Tartan Army reached the group stage of the World Cup six times out of seven between 1974 and 1998 and only twice in that period for the European finals. The first time they returned to the finals in this century was at UEFA EURO 2020. Yet again the group stage was the end of the road.

Scotland showed the value of continuity by keeping faith with Clarke, despite the failure to qualify for the World Cup finals in 2022. Midfield energy personified by the performances and goals of John McGinn and Scott McTominay drove Scotland through to Germany via a complex group featuring former double champions

ABOVE: Scotland have reached the finals for the second time in succession and the fourth occasion overall. They have yet to go beyond the group stage.

SCOTLAND
at the UEFA European Championship

1960	Did not enter
1964	Did not enter
1968	Did not qualify
1972	Did not qualify
1976	Did not qualify
1980	Did not qualify
1984	Did not qualify
1988	Did not qualify
1992	Group stage
1996	Group stage
2000	Did not qualify
2004	Did not qualify
2008	Did not qualify
2012	Did not qualify
2016	Did not qualify
2020*	Group stage

*2020 finals were played in 2021

COACH

STEVE CLARKE

Steve Clarke is now a EURO veteran after leading the Tartan Army to the finals for the second successive time. Clarke, 60, launched his career as a solid, reliable defender with St Mirren before spending 11 years and more than 400 matches with English Premier League side Chelsea. He won the UEFA Cup Winners' Cup, domestic League Cup and FA Cup with the Blues while also playing six times for Scotland. He managed West Bromwich Albion, Reading, Aston Villa and Kilmarnock back in Scotland before succeeding Alex McLeish as national team manager in May 2019.

KEY PLAYER

JOHN McGINN

POSITION: Midfield
CLUB: Aston Villa FC (ENGLAND)
AGE: 29
BORN: 18 October 1994, Glasgow
INTERNATIONAL DEBUT: 29 March 2016 vs Denmark
CAPS: 62 · **GOALS**: 18

John McGinn was voted Scottish Football Writers' International player of the year for a fourth year in a row on the way to UEFA EURO 2024. The Aston Villa midfielder had captained both Scotland's Under-19s and Under-21s before making his senior debut in a 1-0 win over Denmark. He was Scotland's leading scorer with seven goals in the EURO 2020 qualifiers including a first career hat-trick in a win over San Marino. McGinn won his 50th cap in a 2-1 win over the Republic of Ireland in September 2022. At club level McGinn spent three seasons at both St Mirren and Hibernian. He won the Scottish League Cup with St Mirren and the Scottish Cup with Hibs before joining Villa in 2018 and leading them back up into the English Premier League.

Spain, Erling Haaland's Norway, Georgia and Cyprus.

McGinn and McTominay (two) scored the goals in an opening 3-0 win over Cyprus at Scotland's traditional fortress of Hampden Park and Manchester United's McTominay doubled up again in the next 2-0 home win over Spain. Scotland fell behind in Norway to a Haaland strike before snatching victory with two goals in three closing minutes from Lyndon Dykes and Kenny McLean. McTominay scored again in successive wins home to Georgia and away to Cyprus.

Scotland suffered a first defeat, 2-0, in Spain in early October, but it proved academic. Three days later Norway's defeat by Spain handed Scotland their ticket to the finals. Scotland had come through to EURO 2020 via the play-offs, so this was the first time they had qualified directly for any final tournament since 1997.

McGinn and McTominay may have grabbed headlines with their goals but Scotland's progress was an all-round team effort. Clarke varied tactics between 3-4-3 or 3-4-2-1 and 5-3-2, though always with a solid defensive and midfield pack to both protect goalkeeper Angus Gunn and turn defence swiftly into attack.

So-called 'Anglos' have always been important for Scotland. This time around they have a Premier League nucleus in Andrew Robertson (Liverpool), Scott McKenna (Nottingham Forest), McGinn (Aston Villa) and Ryan Christie (Bournemouth), plus three from the English second tier in Gunn (Norwich), defender Ryan Porteous (Watford) and Lyndon Dykes (QPR).

Above all, once more, there were Scotland's fans. Manager Clarke and captain Robertson both paid tribute. Clarke commented: "I said after EURO 2020 that we wanted to be serial qualifiers again and this shows the progress we've had. Our fans have made Hampden Park a place to be feared once again and played a key part in our success, both home and away." As Robertson added: "We look forward to seeing them in Germany in their tens of thousands."

DID YOU KNOW?

Scotland's goalkeeper-captain Robert Gardner played in attack in vain in the second half of the historic first international against England in 1872. The game still ended 0-0.

GROUP A
HUNGARY

Hungary enter the finals for the third successive time hoping to emulate the round of 16 progress in 2016 after a group stage exit three years ago. Coach Marco Rossi has spent six years building the squad who rewarded his faith by reaching Germany with a game to spare.

The all-important goal that secured Hungary's presence in Germany was in fact an own goal, but no one could dispute the right of Rossi's men to return to the finals.

Hungary ended up winning qualifying Group G unbeaten and with a commanding four-point lead over Serbia whom they had beaten 2-1 in successive ties in Belgrade and then Budapest. Ferencváros forward Barnabás Varga scored both home and away. He was on the scoresheet again, in addition to a Dominik Szoboszlai penalty, when Hungary drew 2-2 in Lithuania before undertaking their decisive trip to Bulgaria.

Hungary, playing behind closed doors in Sofia, took an early lead through Martin Ádám after a free-kick from Szoboszlai then fell behind to strikes in each half from Spas Delev and Kiril Despodov (penalty). The draw was secured when Alex Petkov headed a Szoboszlai corner into his own net.

The Hungarian national team have played a historic role in the history of international competition. They played Austria in the first official national team contest on the European continent in 1902 and were runners-up in the Central European Cup of Nations, a forerunner of the UEFA European Championship, in the 1930s and then winners in 1953.

ABOVE: Hungary will be appearing at the UEFA EURO finals tournament for the third time in succession after a gap of more than four decades.

HUNGARY at the UEFA European Championship

1960	Did not qualify
1964	Third place
1968	Did not qualify
1972	Fourth place
1976	Did not qualify
1980	Did not qualify
1984	Did not qualify
1988	Did not qualify
1992	Did not qualify
1996	Did not qualify
2000	Did not qualify
2004	Did not qualify
2008	Did not qualify
2012	Did not qualify
2016	Round of 16
2020*	Group stage

*2020 finals were played in 2021

COACH
MARCO ROSSI

Marco Rossi enjoyed a highly respected 17-year career as a defender in his native Italy as well as abroad in both Mexico and Germany. Notably he won the Coppa Italia with Sampdoria. Rossi retired into a coaching career in 2000. He led six Italian clubs before moving to Hungary in 2012 as head coach with Budapest Honvéd. Rossi had two spells with Honvéd, winning the league title in 2017. He also managed Slovakia's DAC Dunajská Streda before returning to Hungary as national coach in 2018. He guided Hungary successfully through the play-offs to the finals of UEFA EURO 2020.

KEY PLAYER

ATTILA SZALAI

POSITION: Defender
CLUB: TSG Hoffenheim (GERMANY)
AGE: 29
BORN: 20 January 1998, Budapest
INTERNATIONAL DEBUT: 15 November 2019 vs Uruguay
CAPS: 41 • **GOALS**: 1

The consistency and defensive reliability of Attila Szalai has been a significant factor in Hungary's progress to their second successive UEFA EURO. Szalai began his senior professional career with Rapid Vienna then returned to Hungary with Mezőkövesd before transferring in quick succession to Cyprus, Türkiye and Germany with Apollon Limassol, Fenerbahçe and Hoffenheim. He scored three goals in 37 appearances for Hungary's age group teams before being named by coach Marco Rossi for his senior debut as a substitute against Uruguay in 2019. Szalai had been playing his club football for Fenerbahçe when his solid performances earned him starting roles in all three of Hungary's matches at the pandemic-delayed EURO 2020.

Hungary, in the 1930s, were renowned for their coaching expertise, which they exported across the continent and to South America. Then the early 1950s brought the heyday of the Magical Magyars, led by Ferenc Puskás. They won not only the Central European Cup but the Olympic Games gold medal in 1952 and lost only one international in five years before falling short at the one match prized above all others, the FIFA World Cup final in 1954.

Stars such as Puskás, Sándor Kocsis and József Bozsik still rank among the greatest footballers of all time. In 1953, Hungary's Magical Magyars became the first non-British Isles side to beat England at home, winning 6-3 on a legendary occasion at Wembley. Deep-lying forward Nándor Hidegkuti scored a hat-trick.

In the 1960s new stars emerged such as Florian Albert and Ferenc Bene, who led Hungary to the 1962 and 1966 World Cup quarter-finals and Olympic gold in 1964 and 1968. They were also semi-finalists at the original European Championship format in both 1964 and 1972. Hungary appeared intermittently at the finals of subsequent FIFA World Cups but did not reclaim a place at the closing stages of the EURO until reaching the round of 16 in France in 2016.

The latest stars to wear the famous cherry-red shirts feature an experienced core of players who have honed their skills and international experience playing club football not only at home but around the world in Cyprus, England, France, Germany, Italy, Korea Republic, Switzerland, Türkiye and the United States.

Péter Gulácsi and Dénes Dibusz have been vying for the goalkeeping slot over the past decade while defensive colleagues such as Attila Szalai, Willi Orban, Ádám Lang, Loïc Négo and Endre Botka boast more than 250 international appearances between them. In midfield Pisa's Ádám Nagy has amassed around 80 caps in eight years, but the outstanding creative force on whom Hungary will rely in Germany is Szoboszlai. Varga and the Liverpool star were Hungary's four-goal joint leading scorers during their qualifying march to the finals.

DID YOU KNOW?

Hungary were beaten semi-finalists twice in the early days of the championship but then had to wait 44 years before returning to the finals in 2016.

GROUP A
SWITZERLAND

Consistency is the watchword for Switzerland on the international stage. They are returning to the finals of the UEFA EURO for the fifth time in six tournaments. The next target is to progress beyond the last eight. Three years ago Spain denied them a semi-finals place only after a penalty shoot-out.

While Switzerland has long been known as the host to the administrative headquarters of both European federation UEFA in Nyon and world governing body FIFA in Zurich, La Nati have really come of age on the international scene in recent years out on the pitch.

They have appeared at the EURO tournament on five occasions with a best quarter-finals placing last time around, and have reached the finals of the World Cup on 12 occasions, with a best finish in the quarter-finals three times.

Switzerland's return to the top table of the European international game was achieved via the runners-up slot in qualifying Group I. They lost only one of their ten matches and were also top scorers in the group with 22 goals. Five came in an opening victory away to Belarus and three apiece at home to Israel, Andorra and Belarus.

However, qualification was not secured until the penultimate matchday and a nervy 1-1 home draw against Kosovo. Switzerland dominated possession but had to wait until two minutes after half-time before a Ruben Vargas header broke down Kosovo's defensive resistance. Kosovo levelled through Muhamet Hyseni in the closing stages but the point was sufficient to guarantee Switzerland a ticket to the finals.

ABOVE: Switzerland have contested the UEFA EURO finals on five occasions, with a best finish as quarter-finalists in the 2020 competition.

SWITZERLAND at the UEFA European Championship

1960	Did not qualify
1964	Did not qualify
1968	Did not qualify
1972	Did not qualify
1976	Did not qualify
1980	Did not qualify
1984	Did not qualify
1988	Did not qualify
1992	Did not qualify
1996	Group stage
2000	Did not qualify
2004	Group stage
2008	Group stage
2012	Did not qualify
2016	Round of 16
2020*	Quarter-finals

*2020 finals were played in 2021

COACH

MURAT YAKIN

Murat Yakin, who played 49 times in central defence for Switzerland between 1994 and 2004, was appointed national team coach in succession to Vladimir Petković after UEFA EURO 2020. His club playing career took him to Grasshoppers, Germany's VfB Stuttgart and Kaiserslautern, Türkiye's Fenerbahçe then five more years back home in Basel. Yakin's club coaching career has been undertaken almost entirely in Switzerland with Thun, Luzern, Basel, Schaffhausen, Grasshoppers and Sion apart from a year in Russia with Spartak Moskva. Younger brother Hakan Yakin was also a Swiss international.

KEY PLAYER

XHERDAN SHAQIRI

POSITION: Forward
CLUB: Chicago Fire FC (USA)
AGE: 32
BORN: 10 October 1991, Gjilan, Kosovo
INTERNATIONAL DEBUT: 3 March 2010 vs Uruguay
CAPS: 119 • **GOALS**: 29

Xherdan Shaqiri was born in what was then Yugoslavia to Kosovar Albanian parents who emigrated to Switzerland in 1992. He made his Under-21s debut in 2009 and senior debut a year later. Since then Shaqiri has been a fixture in midfield or attack for all Switzerland's appearances in major tournaments. These included UEFA EURO 2016 and 2020, when Switzerland lost on penalties to Spain in the quarter-finals. In November 2021, Shaqiri became only the fifth Swiss player to reach 100 caps. At club level he won three Swiss league titles with Basel before leaving for Bayern München, Italy's Internazionale then England's Stoke City and Liverpool. Shaqiri's three years at Anfield included title triumphs in the UEFA Champions League, FIFA Club World Cup and English Premier League.

Switzerland could have wrapped up their campaign on top of the table had they won their final match in Romania. Instead they lost 1-0. Even so, they still ended a safe two points ahead of third-placed Israel. Switzerland's Zeki Amdouni was the group's six-goal top scorer. The 23-year-old who plays for Burnley in the English Premier League was now firmly established in the Swiss squad after briefly representing his father's Turkish homeland at Under-21 level.

The Swiss game owes much to a historic British influence as evidenced by club names such as Grasshoppers and Young Boys. Those early days saw Switzerland finish as runners-up at the 1924 Olympic Games football tournament. They excelled on the world stage, inspired by the Abegglen brothers, Max and André, who scored more than 60 goals between them. Sharing responsibility was Austrian master coach Karl Rappan. He devised the 'Swiss Bolt' defensive system and guided Switzerland to the finals of the World Cup on four occasions.

After 1966 the national side suffered a reversal of fortunes and failed to qualify for anything until returning to the world stage in 1994 under English manager Roy Hodgson. They made their EURO debut two years later. Since 2004 Switzerland have been missing from the finals of the two major national team tournaments only once, the EURO in 2012.

The squad who brought the Swiss safely through to Germany included familiar names such as veteran goalkeeper Yann Sommer, wingback Ricardo Rodriguez and central defender Manuel Akanji, who had been enjoying an outstanding season with European and English club champions Manchester City. Captain and anchor at the heart of midfield was Granit Xhaka, with attacking creativity on either wing being provided by the similarly experienced Xherdan Shaqiri. Both men have played well over 100 times for their country, just the sort of consistency which keeps Switzerland among the European elite.

DID YOU KNOW?

Switzerland failed to reach the finals at their first nine attempts but will be present this time for the sixth time in eight tournaments.

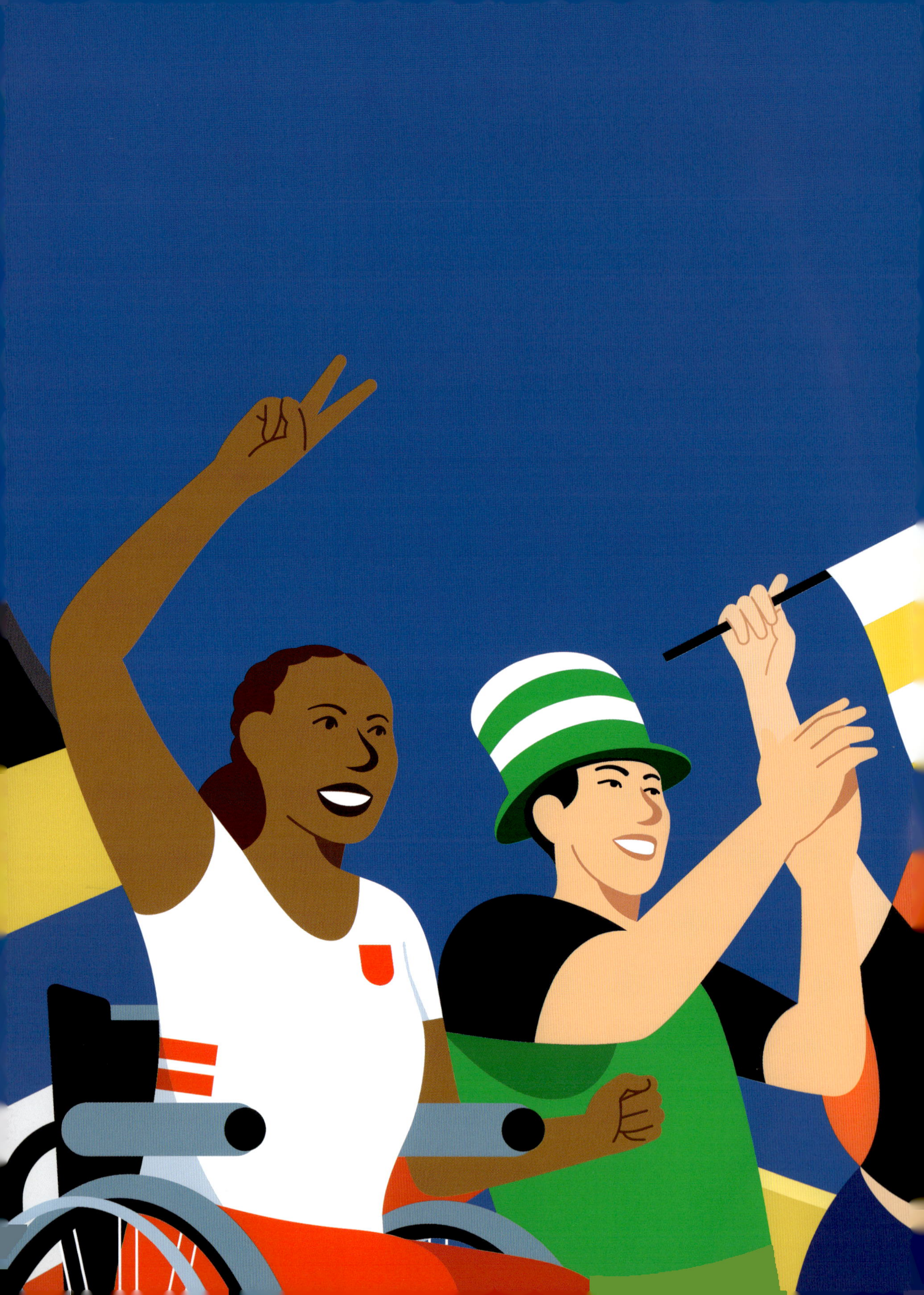

UEFA EURO 2024 GERMANY

GROUP B

Spain have been European champions three times and have been ever-present at the finals since 1996. Defending champions Italy were also winners as hosts in 1968. Croatia have been quarter-finalists twice. Albania are making only their second finals appearance. Spain, Croatia and Italy were all present at UEFA EURO 2020 and were all in the same group at EURO 2012.

- Spain
- Croatia
- Italy
- Albania

GROUP B
SPAIN

Spain will be appearing at the EURO finals for the 12th time. They have missed out only once since 1980 and triumphed on a record-equalling three occasions. La Roja will always be among the favourites for any tournament, as befits a nation who also boast FIFA World Cup success.

Spain paraded the youngest EURO 2024 squad among the main title contenders, with an average age of 25. The team put together by manager Luis de la Fuente featured many of the players who have grown up in a variety of successful age group competitions. De la Fuente knew them well after a decade with the Under-19s and Under-21s.

The 62-year-old had succeeded Luis Enrique after Spain's dramatic exits in penalty shoot-outs against Italy at the EURO semi-finals in 2021 and then against Morocco in the round of 16 at the 2022 World Cup.

Spain took off in qualifying Group A with a 3-0 win over Norway thanks to two late goals in just over a minute from Joselu. But a 2-0 defeat in Scotland set early alarm bells ringing. The fixtures schedule in a five-team group saw Spain fall back before their return to the fray last September.

Five days was all it took to ease nerves with 13 goals in two wins. First captain Álvaro Morata scored a hat-trick in a 7-1 win away to Georgia then Ferran Torres struck twice in a 6-0 home win over Cyprus. Spain followed up with a 2-0 home win over Scotland and 1-0 victory against Norway on a chilly night in Oslo which secured their place in the finals with two games to spare. Morata had a

ABOVE: Spain, champions on three occasions and semi-finalists at EURO 2020, are in the finals for the twelfth time, only one fewer than Germany.

SPAIN
at the UEFA European Championship

1960	Withdrew
1964	WINNERS
1968	Did not qualify
1972	Did not qualify
1976	Did not qualify
1980	Group stage
1984	Runners-up
1988	Group stage
1992	Did not qualify
1996	Quarter-finals
2000	Quarter-finals
2004	Group stage
2008	WINNERS
2012	WINNERS
2016	Round of 16
2020*	Semi-finals

*2020 finals were played in 2021

COACH

LUIS DE LA FUENTE

Luis de la Fuente achieved a successful career as Spain's youth team manager before being appointed to follow Luis Enrique after the FIFA World Cup in Qatar. He accomplished immediate success by guiding Spain to victory in the 2023 UEFA Nations League. Many of De la Fuente's current senior squad played under his management in winning both the European Under-19 and Under-21 titles in 2015 and 2019 respectively. He also led the Olympic team to a silver medal in the delayed Games in 2021. De la Fuente's 13-year playing career included a league and cup double with Athletic Club.

KEY PLAYER

ÁLVARO MORATA

POSITION: Forward
CLUB: Club Atlético de Madrid (SPAIN)
AGE: 31
BORN: 23 October 1992, Madrid
INTERNATIONAL DEBUT: 15 November 2014 vs Belarus
CAPS: 69 • **GOALS**: 34

Álvaro Morata, Spain's captain, has been scoring goals for his country since long before his senior debut in 2014. Morata was top scorer at the UEFA European Under-19 Championship finals in 2011 and again at the U21s in 2013. His senior goals included the winner against Sweden which sent Spain to the 2022 FIFA World Cup finals. Morata launched his senior career at hometown club Real Madrid, with whom he won eight trophies in two spells including the UEFA Champions League twice and the UEFA Super Cup. More honours followed in England at Chelsea, in Italy with Juventus and back home with Atlético.

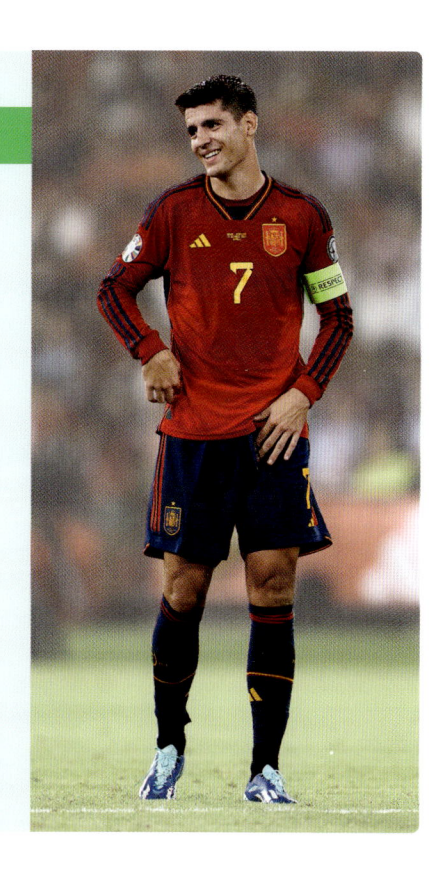

first-half 'goal' disallowed by VAR but the technology was on Spain's side when Barcelona midfielder Gavi struck the second-half winner.

De la Fuente hailed his "team of the future" and added: "Spanish football always has been among the elite and now I think we are going to make our fans happy. There's a long way to go, a lot to improve but we have a fantastic foundation."

That foundation was a squad featuring, by contrast with other eras, a mix of players from a variety of clubs at home and abroad. This meant four players each from Real Madrid and Real Sociedad, two from Barcelona and Athletic Club, one each from Sevilla, Osasuna, Atlético and Granada plus half a dozen from England, France and Saudi Arabia.

Spain had made their international debut at the Olympic Games in Antwerp in 1920 then reached the quarter-finals of both the 1928 Olympics and 1934 World Cup with a team starring legendary goalkeeper Ricardo Zamora.

El Clásico rivals Real Madrid and Barcelona brought glamour and glory to the early years of European club competition in the 1950s, inspired by imported talent such as Argentinian Alfredo Di Stéfano and Hungarians Ferenc Puskás and László Kubala.

They inspired new home-grown heroes. Barcelona playmaker Luis Suárez and Madrid winger Amancio starred in the Spain team who won their first European crown in 1964. A two-decade drought was ended by quarter-finals progress at the World Cup in 1986 then Olympic Games gold in Barcelona in 1992.

Spain surpassed all of this when their 'tiki taka' possession game brought a four-year monopoly of the major prizes. Xavi Hernández, Andrés Iniesta, Iker Casillas and Co earned victories, 1-0 over Germany at EURO 2008, 1-0 over the Netherlands at the 2010 World Cup then 4-0 over Italy at EURO 2012. De la Fuente and his "team of the future" must believe a return to the podium is overdue.

DID YOU KNOW?

Spain's victory over the Soviet Union in the 1964 final at the Estadio Santiago Bernabéu in Madrid was witnessed by the highest official attendance of any EURO match at 79,115.

GROUP B
CROATIA

Croatia gained independence after the break-up of Yugoslavia in the early 1990s. The following 30 years have seen the iconic red-and-white shirts sparkle on every significant stage but without a trophy to reward their consistency. Perhaps UEFA EURO 2024 can deliver the breakthrough.

The story of the dramatic footballing rise of Croatia out of the social and political upheaval of the late 1980s and early 1990s is remarkable, even considering their central role in the achievements of the former Yugoslavia. An independent national football federation was granted membership of FIFA in 1992 and of UEFA a year later. The national team then reached the quarter-finals on their main stage debut at EURO '96.

Two years later Croatia marked their debut at the FIFA World Cup finals by finishing third and seeing forward Davor Šuker hailed as the tournament's six-goal leading marksman. Other key players included playmakers Zvonimir Boban and Robert Prosinečki. All three had been world youth champions with the former Yugoslavia in 1987.

Since then Croatia have been regular contenders at the finals of both the World Cup and the EURO. They have been absent from the World Cup finals only in 2010 and the EURO only in 2000.

More often they have been present in the all-important, high-tension closing stages. This included a shoot-out defeat in the quarter-finals at EURO 2008, round of 16 in 2016, then the highest peak so far as runners-up at the 2018 World Cup. By now Šuker had progressed from leading the

ABOVE: Croatia have never progressed beyond their two quarter-finals exits in six appearances at the UEFA EURO finals since their debut in 1996.

CROATIA at the UEFA European Championship

1960	No national team
1964	No national team
1968	No national team
1972	No national team
1976	No national team
1980	No national team
1984	No national team
1988	No national team
1992	No national team
1996	Quarter-finals
2000	Did not qualify
2004	Group stage
2008	Quarter-finals
2012	Group stage
2016	Round of 16
2020*	Round of 16

*2020 finals were played in 2021

COACH
ZLATKO DALIĆ

Zlatko Dalić boasts a remarkable record as one of the longest-serving of the current national team coaches. Dalić, 57, was appointed in October 2017 to rescue Croatia's FIFA World Cup qualifying campaign. He not only led them to Russia but on to a runners-up finish. He took Croatia to the round of 16 at UEFA EURO 2020, third place at the World Cup in Qatar and runners-up at the UEFA Nations League. Dalić had built his reputation with Croatia's Under-21s between 2006 and 2011. At club level he coached several domestic sides in Albania, including Dinamo Tirana, and then in Saudi Arabia and in the United Arab Emirates with Al-Ain.

KEY PLAYER

DOMINIK LIVAKOVIĆ

POSITION: Goalkeeper
CLUB: Fenerbahçe SK (TÜRKIYE)
AGE: 29
BORN: 9 January 1995, Zadar
INTERNATIONAL DEBUT: 11 January 2017 vs Chile
CAPS: 51 • **GOALS**: 0

Dominik Livaković earned international acclaim with his heroics as Croatia finished third at the 2022 FIFA World Cup in Qatar. Livaković saved the most penalties both in one shoot-out as well as overall across the tournament. In the round of 16 Livaković saved three times against Japan and then followed up by foiling Rodrygo in the quarter-final shoot-out defeat of Brazil. He thus equalled the tournament record of four shoot-out saves. Before making his senior debut in 2017, Livaković had played 34 times for Croatia at youth levels from Under-15s to Under-21s. His club career began with NK Zagreb and he later won six Croatia league titles and five other major domestic trophies with neighbours Dinamo. Livaković transferred to Türkiye's Fenerbahçe last summer.

attack to leading the federation. Next came the round of 16 at EURO 2020, third place at the 2022 World Cup, then runners-up at the UEFA Nations League last year.

Central to all the latter achievements has been a determined nucleus including Danijel Subašić and then Dominik Livaković in goal, Dejan Lovren and Domagoj Vida in central defence and the apparently timeless and tireless Luka Modrić at the heart of attacking creativity. Long-serving coach Zlatko Dalić has surrounded and supported the nucleus of the team with a steady supply of committed defenders, midfielders, direct wingers and aggressive forwards.

In defence, Joško Gvardiol continued to progress into an international star after an outstanding World Cup in Qatar while Mateo Kovačić, Marcelo Brozović and Mario Pašalić brought skill and strength to midfield. Veterans Andrej Kramarić and Ante Budimir ran as hard as ever up front.

Reaching Germany and the finals of EURO 2024 was hard work, however, in Group D which included Türkiye, Wales as well as Armenia and Latvia. They were disappointed to open with a 1-1 home draw against Wales, then closed the spring campaign with a solid 2-0 win in Türkiye with two first-half goals from midfielder Kovačić.

Last September brought victories at home to Latvia and away to Armenia but there followed two defeats – by a 1-0 scoreline at home to Türkiye and then 2-1 in Wales. Croatia thus approached their last two fixtures level on points with Wales. With two fixtures remaining, the prize at stake was the runners-up spot behind Türkiye and automatic qualification.

The first hurdle was overcome when early goals from Lovro Majer and Kramarić secured a 2-0 win against Latvia in Riga. This meant Croatia had to win at home to Armenia to ensure they finished ahead of Wales. Modrić pulled all the strings in midfield and Budimir's second international goal, a close-range header, delivered a 1-0 victory and the ticket to Germany.

DID YOU KNOW?

Croatia are appearing in Germany at the EURO for the seventh time, having missed out only once since joining the European federation in 1993.

GROUP B
ITALY

Italy, reigning champions of Europe, have not prospered since victory at Wembley in July 2021. The Azzurri missed out on the last FIFA World Cup and then edged into UEFA EURO 2024 thanks to a better head-to-head record against Ukraine after they finished level on points.

This will not prevent Italy from being hailed among the most dangerous contenders when they arrive in Germany. History speaks for itself. Italy have won the World Cup four times and their EURO victory three years ago was the second in their history. Italy were also runners-up in 2000 and 2012, fourth in 1980 and 1988 and quarter-finalists twice.

Both Italy's appearances in the final have been tense affairs. In 1968 they defeated the former Yugoslavia 2-0 in a Rome replay on goals from Luigi Riva and Pietro Anastasi. In 2021 they achieved a 1-1 draw with final hosts England and triumphed on penalties. Goalkeeper Gianluigi Donnarumma was the hero, saving the last kick from Bukayo Saka.

Coach Roberto Mancini's team extended their world record for the longest unbeaten run to 37 matches before finally losing 2-1 to Spain in a UEFA Nations League semi-final in Milan in October 2021. This was Italy's first competitive home defeat since 1999 and the record filled fans with 2022 World Cup optimism. Instead, Italy lost to North Macedonia in a play-off semi-final and did not make it to Qatar.

Italy faced a tough Group C in the EURO qualifiers which included Ukraine and, yet again, England, to whom they lost their opening tie 2-1 at home. A 2-0 win in Malta three days later, with

ITALY
at the UEFA European Championship

1960	Did not enter
1964	Did not qualify
1968	WINNERS
1972	Did not qualify
1976	Did not qualify
1980	Fourth place
1984	Did not qualify
1988	Fourth place
1992	Did not qualify
1996	Group stage
2000	Runners-up
2004	Group stage
2008	Quarter-finals
2012	Runners-up
2016	Quarter-finals
2020*	WINNERS

*2020 finals were played in 2021

COACH

LUCIANO SPALLETTI

Luciano Spalletti had an immediate effect on the Azzurri, guiding them safely through to UEFA EURO 2024 only three months after having been appointed in succession to Roberto Mancini. Spalletti, 65, played in the lower leagues before launching his coaching career with Empoli in 1993. Spells with Sampdoria, Venezia, Udinese and Ancona earned a contract at Roma. Here he won the Coppa Italia twice and then followed up with two Russian league titles with Zenit Saint Petersburg. Back home, Spalletti had two seasons with Internazionale before leading Napoli to the Serie A crown in 2022/23.

ABOVE: Italy have competed at the UEFA EURO finals on ten occasions, winning the title twice and finishing as runners-up in two campaigns.

KEY PLAYER

JORGINHO

POSITION: Midfielder
CLUB: Arsenal FC (ENGLAND)
AGE: 32
BORN: 20 December 1991, Imbituba, Brazil
INTERNATIONAL DEBUT: 24 March 2016 vs Spain
CAPS: 50 • **GOALS**: 5

Jorginho was hailed as the UEFA Player of the Year in 2021 after winning UEFA EURO 2020 with Italy and the UEFA Champions League with Chelsea. Italy's midfield anchor (full name Jorge Luiz Frello Filho) had been born in Brazil and was only 15 when he joined Italy's Hellas Verona. In 2014 he transferred to Napoli and won both the Coppa Italia and Supercoppa under coach Maurizio Sarri. In 2018 he followed Sarri to the English Premier League and Chelsea, with whom he won the UEFA Europa League in 2019 and then that Champions League crown. Jorginho, who qualified to play for Italy through his grandfather, opted for the Azzurri in 2014 and made his senior international debut two years later.

goals from Mateo Retegui and Matteo Pessina, proved their last competitive match under Mancini. In August he stepped down and the federation brought in Luciano Spalletti, fresh from his Serie A triumph with Napoli.

Spalletti's Italy started decisively. The team secured an important 1-1 draw in North Macedonia then defeated Ukraine 2-1 in Milan. Those two first-half goals from Internazionale midfielder Davide Frattesi proved crucial not only on the night but also when the rivals drew 0-0 in the concluding tie.

The situation in Ukraine saw the match staged in Leverkusen, Germany. Italy survived a VAR check for a Ukraine penalty claim in the final moments to secure a goalless draw. UEFA's qualifying tournament rules and regulations set mutual results as the first dividing factor for teams level on points. Thus Italy, courtesy of that initial victory over Ukraine, qualified for the finals as group runners-up.

Spalletti said: "We can take a moment to pat ourselves on the back. From here the level will step up. Now, the fun begins."

Italy prepare for the fun with a new-look defence. Donnarumma, player of the tournament at EURO 2020, remains the goalkeeping cornerstone. Remarkably, for all his achievements, the Paris Saint-Germain star is still only 25. In front of him, however, Italy can no longer look to old heroes Giorgio Chiellini and Leonardo Bonucci. Inter veteran Francesco Acerbi and Torino newcomer Alessandro Buongiorno stepped up to fill the gap for the qualifying climax.

Midfield provides the heartbeat of the team. Jorginho and Nicola Barella have both made more than 50 appearances for Italy, who can also call on important experience from Bryan Cristante and Marco Verratti. Up front the search for goals is more intriguing. The only squad member from the EURO qualifiers to have managed double figures for Italy was Lazio's 34-year-old Ciro Immobile.

But then, as Italy proved three years ago, they can call on goals from all over the pitch: no fewer than seven different men delivered their title-winning goals at EURO 2020.

DID YOU KNOW?

Italy are making their 11th appearance at the UEFA EURO and, once qualified, have only twice failed to progress beyond the group stages.

GROUP B
ALBANIA

Albania are appearing at a major tournament for just the second time after their debut at UEFA EURO 2016. They failed only narrowly to reach the round of 16 then, so now, after topping their qualifying group, the target is progress to the knockout stages for the first time.

South American knowhow contributed to Albania's success in qualifying top of Group E, because national coach Sylvinho is Brazilian and assistants include a compatriot in Doriva plus the former Argentinian international star Pablo Zabaleta.

They flew in to start their Albanian adventure in January last year and repair squad morale after the players fell short in the FIFA World Cup qualifying campaign. Albania now faced a tough European challenge in a group featuring World Cup qualifiers in Czechia and Poland.

Albania lost only one match, their first, 1-0 in Poland. They then put together a sequence of four wins and three draws including a 2-0 defeat of Poland back in Tirana. They followed up with their most decisive victory, 3-0, at home to Czechia with two goals from Taulant Seferi and one from Korea-based Jasir Asani.

Seferi holds a record as the youngest player to feature in a full international for North Macedonia, where he was born, before taking up Albanian citizenship in 2017.

Albania secured their place at the finals, top of the table and with a game to spare, after a 1-1 draw away to Moldova. Sokol Cikalleshi opened the scoring with a penalty after Seferi had been fouled. Keeper Etrit Berisha was beaten only in the closing minutes. Back

ABOVE: Albania entered the UEFA EURO qualifying tournament on 13 previous occasions, reaching the finals only once before, in 2016.

ALBANIA at the UEFA European Championship

1960	Did not enter
1964	Did not qualify
1968	Did not qualify
1972	Did not qualify
1976	Did not enter
1980	Did not enter
1984	Did not qualify
1988	Did not qualify
1992	Did not qualify
1996	Did not qualify
2000	Did not qualify
2004	Did not qualify
2008	Did not qualify
2012	Did not qualify
2016	Group stage
2020*	Did not qualify

*2020 finals were played in 2021

COACH

SYLVINHO

Sylvinho knows all about success on the big European stage. In 2006 and 2009, then playing as a left-back, he was a UEFA Champions League winner with Barcelona. This was the pinnacle of the playing career of Sylvio Mendes Campos Júnior (his full name). He also played for Brazil's Corinthians, England's Arsenal and Manchester City as well as Spain's Celta de Vigo before turning to coaching. Spells on the staff of Italy's Internazionale and Brazil preceded coaching contracts with Lyon in France and his old club, Corinthians. Sylvinho was appointed by Albania in January last year.

KEY PLAYER

ETRIT BERISHA

POSITION: Goalkeeper
CLUB: Empoli FC (ITALY)
AGE: 35
BORN: 10 March 1989, Pristina, Kosovo
INTERNATIONAL DEBUT: 27 May 2012 vs Iran
CAPS: 80 · **GOALS**: 0

Etrit Berisha was born in Kosovo but qualified for Albania through family background and made his debut under then national coach Gianni De Biasi in 2012. His safe handling and command of the penalty box enabled Berisha to establish himself as his country's No1. Four years later he was one of the heroes of Albania's appearance at UEFA EURO 2016. Berisha began his career in Kosovo, then moved to Sweden as a teenager with Kalmar. He was Swedish league goalkeeper of the year in 2013 before heading to Italy with Lazio. Further transfers took him to Atalanta, SPAL, Torino and then to Empoli last August. Berisha boasts a successful record for not only saving penalty kicks but also for converting them.

in Tirana, Albania fans poured out on to the streets to celebrate qualification.

A goalless home draw against Faroe Islands ensured Albania finished top, level on points with Czechia and ahead of them on mutual results.

Sylvinho said: "This is a dream, a beautiful thing. Unbelievable. We did a great job. Everyone, together." Prime Minister Edi Rama duly presented Sylvinho with the golden eagle decoration awarded for outstanding civic service to the nation. Sylvinho was the first non-Albanian thus honoured.

Albania's squad was drawn from clubs in Belgium, Croatia, Czechia, England, Germany, Italy, Korea Republic, Russia, Spain, Sweden, Türkiye and the United Arab Emirates.

The squad boasts a phalanx of highly experienced internationals and a EURO 2016 veteran in goalkeeper Berisha. Defensive commanders Elseid Hysaj and Switzerland-born captain Berat Djimsiti have more than 50 caps. A similar weight of experience features in midfield with Odise Roshi plus Keidi Bare, Klaus Gjasula, Nedim Bajrami and Ylber Ramadani. However, Albania owed much to their new attacking discoveries in Asani and Seferi. Asani and midfielder Bajrami were Albania's joint three-goal leading scorers.

Football arrived in Albania at the start of the 1900s, although a federation was not created until 1932. There was then a further wait until the national team made their debut, against neighbouring Yugoslavia, in 1946. Several outstanding players – Riza Lushta, Loro Borici and Naim Kryeziu – played in Italy in the early 1940s. Then came Panajot Pano, a star of the 1950s and early 1960s whose son also became an international, and subsequently Sulejman Demollari.

By then Albania was emerging from political and sporting isolation and contested qualifying rounds of the EURO and World Cup. Their lack of international experience meant they fell short until EURO 2016, when Albania finally made it to the finals.

In France, a 1-0 victory over Romania in Albania's concluding group match lifted them to third place but it was not quite enough to reach the round of 16. Now to try again.

DID YOU KNOW?

Albania's national team – the 'Red and Blacks' or 'Eagles' – will be competing at a major tournament finals for only the second time, after a debut at UEFA EURO 2016.

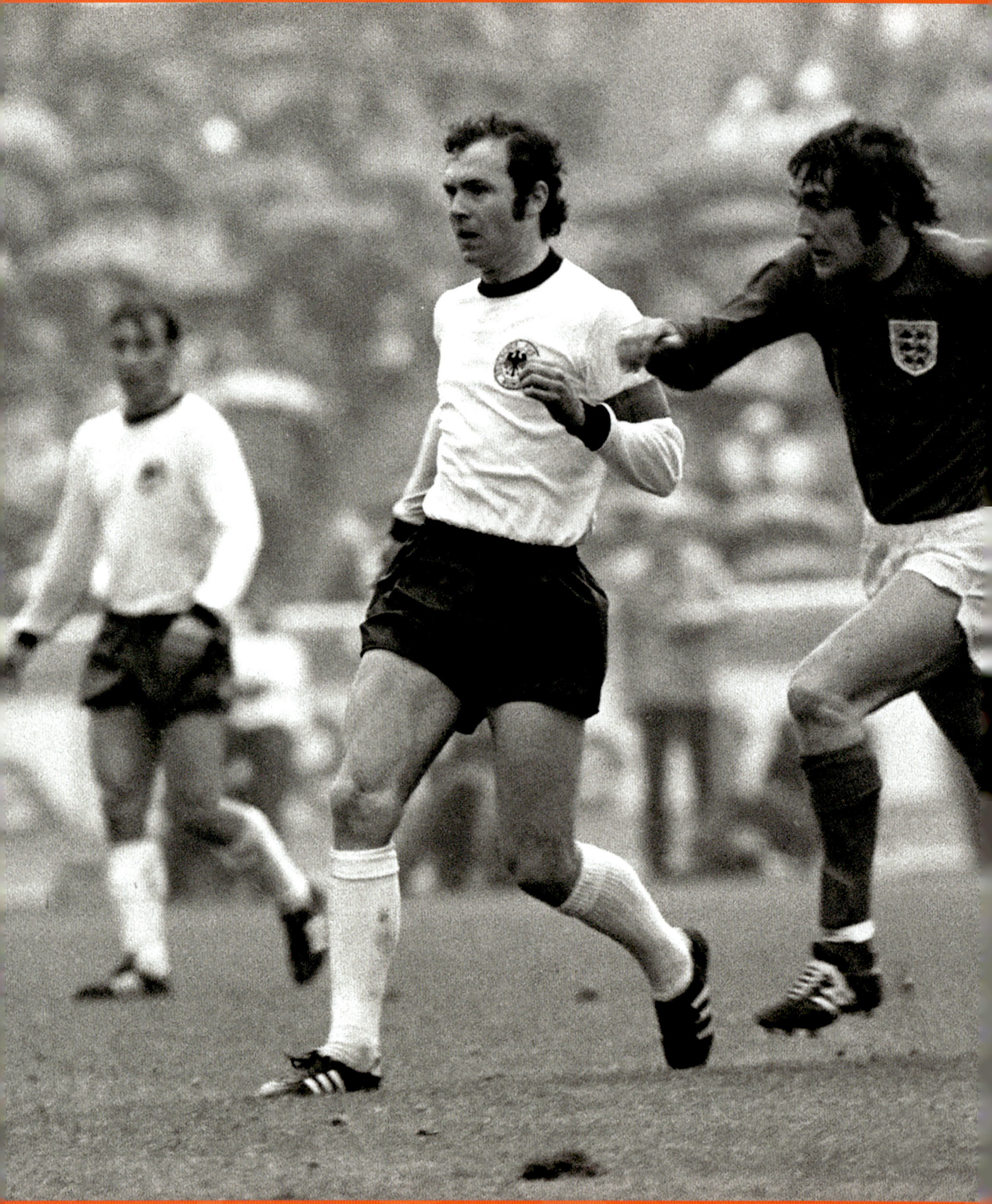

1972

Magic Moments:
BECKENBAUER BREAKTHROUGH

29 APRIL 1972 / WEMBLEY

No senior German national team had won away to England when manager Helmut Schön brought his team to Wembley for the first leg of their EURO quarter-final in 1972. His squad had been weakened by injuries, prompting the introduction of Bayern München youngsters Paul Breitner, Hans-Georg Schwarzenbeck and Uli Hoeness. Yet the brilliant creative combination of libero and captain Franz Beckenbauer with playmaker Günter Netzer inspired a 3-1 victory. Hoeness, Netzer and Gerd Müller scored the goals which inflicted only England's fourth defeat at Wembley by continental opposition. West Germany went on to win their first European crown with a 3-0 victory over the Soviet Union in the final in Brussels. Two years later Beckenbauer and his men would also win the FIFA World Cup.

LEFT: Captain Franz Beckenbauer battles with Norman Hunter as he leads West Germany past England in West Berlin and into the 1972 European Championship semi-finals.

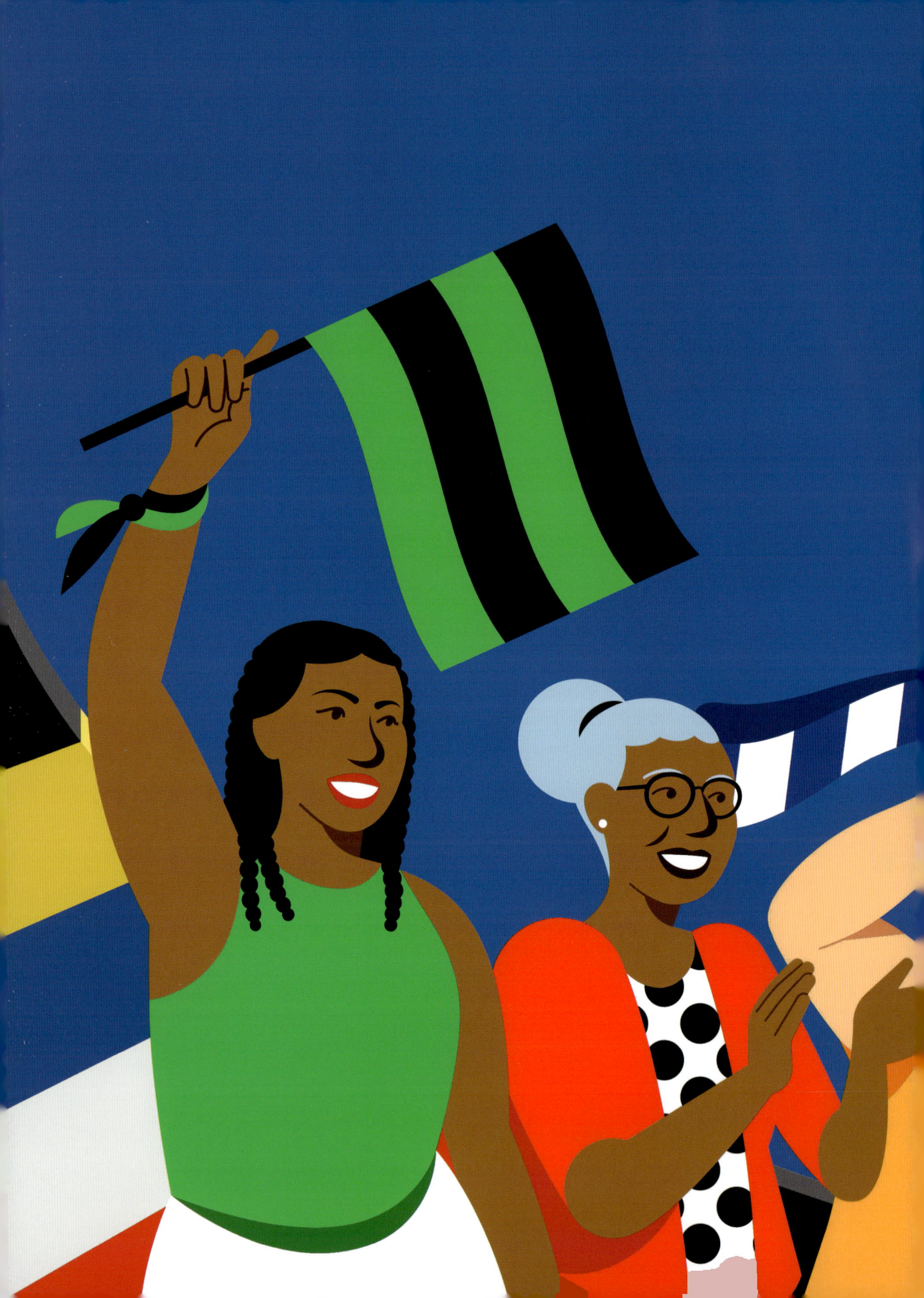

UEFA EURO 2024 GERMANY

GROUP C

Denmark were champions in 1992 and semi-finalists in 1964, 1984 and at EURO 2020. England were runners-up at UEFA EURO 2020 and semi-finalists in 1968 and 1996. Serbia (and Montenegro) were quarter-finalists in 2000. Slovenia are making their second finals appearance. England met Denmark in the semi-finals at EURO 2020.

- Slovenia
- Denmark
- Serbia
- England

GROUP C
SLOVENIA

Slovenia's ambition on their fourth appearance at a major tournament must be to reach the knockout stage, a barrier at UEFA EURO 2020 and their two FIFA World Cups. They can draw confidence from a qualifying campaign which saw them kept off the top of their group only by the head-to-head rule.

Group H presented the formidable challenge of a six-team pool also comprising Denmark, Finland, Kazakhstan, Northern Ireland and San Marino. Slovenia began promisingly in Kazakhstan by recovering from 1-0 down at the interval to claim a 2-1 victory with second-half goals by Norway-based defender David Brekalo from Viking FK and Žan Vipotnik from Bordeaux.

Vipotnik had marked his debut as a substitute in the 70th minute by scoring Slovenia's winning goal just eight minutes later. He thus became the second youngest player, at just 21, to score for Slovenia. Benjamin Šeško, coincidentally the youngest, scored the team's opening goal in their next match, a 2-0 defeat of San Marino. They then closed out the spring campaign with a potentially costly defeat in Finland and a home draw against group favourites Denmark.

Winning form was regained in the autumn before a last-match decider against Kazakhstan. Slovenia, needing at least a draw in Ljubljana, won 2-1 with goals in each half from Šeško (penalty) and Benjamin Verbič. Victory lifted them level on points with Denmark, though in second place on head-to-head results. Slovenia thus returned to the EURO more than 20 years after their only previous appearance in Belgium and

ABOVE: Slovenia appeared in the group stage of the UEFA EURO finals on only their second qualifying attempt, in 2000 in Belgium and the Netherlands.

SLOVENIA at the UEFA European Championship

1960	No national team
1964	No national team
1968	No national team
1972	No national team
1976	No national team
1980	No national team
1984	No national team
1988	No national team
1992	No national team
1996	Did not qualify
2000	Group stage
2004	Did not qualify
2008	Did not qualify
2012	Did not qualify
2016	Did not qualify
2020*	Did not qualify

*2020 finals were played in 2021

COACH

MATJAŽ KEK

Matjaž Kek is in his second spell with the national team. He began his coaching career with home-town Maribor and led them to the league title in 2000 and then again in 2003. Three years later Kek was appointed head coach of the national youth teams. In 2007 he was promoted to head coach of the senior national team and led them to the FIFA World Cup finals in South Africa. Later he coached Al-Ittihad in Saudi Arabia before guiding Rijeka to a Croatia league title and two domestic cups. Kek was reappointed by Slovenia in November 2018, leading them in the UEFA EURO 2020 qualifying campaign.

KEY PLAYER

BENJAMIN ŠEŠKO

POSITION: Forward
CLUB: RB Leipzig (GERMANY)
AGE: 21
BORN: 31 May 2003, Radeče
INTERNATIONAL DEBUT: 1 June 2021 vs North Macedonia
CAPS: 26 • **GOALS**: 10

Benjamin Šeško made a decisive impact with his five goals in Slovenia's UEFA EURO 2024 qualifying campaign. Šeško was born and brought up in the eastern Slovenian region of Radeče and first attracted attention with his goals at youth level as a 15-year-old with NK Krško. His free-scoring form continued after a transfer in 2018 to NK Domžale. A year later he moved into Austrian football with FC Salzburg. Šeško undertook a spell on loan at FC Liefering before making a senior league debut for Salzburg and featuring in their league and cup-winning squad in 2021/22. He was league top scorer and champion again in 2023 before transferring to RB Leipzig. Šeško became Slovenia's then-youngest-ever international when he made his debut aged 18 years and one day in a 1-1 draw against North Macedonia.

---

the Netherlands in 2000. Šeško was their five-goal top scorer.

Coach Matjaž Kek said: "We are happy, delighted and proud. It's well-deserved for this generation of footballers. They have restored faith in Slovene football." UEFA's Slovenian president Aleksander Čeferin described it as "a happy day for Slovenia's football, for Slovenia and Slovenia's sports".

Slovenia, bordered now by modern-day Austria, Croatia, Hungary and Italy, was integrated into the new state of Yugoslavia in 1918. Hence it had no formal national football team, though a regional representative side lost 5-0 to a France Select in 1921. A handful of further such matches were staged before Slovenia separated from Yugoslavia in 1992 and the newly-independent FA duly joined UEFA.

History was made in 2000 when Slovenia made their debut at a major tournament, the EURO in Belgium and the Netherlands. They qualified after defeating Ukraine 3-2 on aggregate in a two-leg play-off. In the finals they led neighbours Serbia and Montenegro 3-0 before conceding three late goals, lost to Spain and were eliminated after a draw with Norway.

Star of the current squad which has ended the two-decade absence from the EURO is goalkeeper Jan Oblak, ranked among the best in the world, from Atlético. His most experienced defensive colleagues include Italian-based Petar Stojanović from Sampdoria and Jaka Bijol from Udinese. In midfield Jasmin Kurtić has played more than 80 times for Slovenia while Verbič has also won more than 50 caps.

Šeško, from RB Leipzig in the German Bundesliga, proved himself in qualifying as Slovenia's newest star in attack while Luka Zahović offers a connection back to the team's European campaign in 2000. His father, Zlatko Zahović, led Slovenia's attack back then and remains the country's 35-goal all-time leading scorer.

DID YOU KNOW?

Slovenia last reached the UEFA EURO for their one and only previous time in 2000, when they were eliminated in the group stage.

GROUP C
DENMARK

Denmark rank among the elite group of ten nations who can draw pride from UEFA European Championship success. The team, coined Danish Dynamite, triumphed in 1992 and successive generations have sought to recreate those glory days. EURO 2024 provides another opportunity to try.

Denmark finished on top of qualifying Group H with a game to spare after they started in style, Rasmus Højlund's hat-trick providing a 3-1 win over Finland. Højlund also scored twice next time out to provide Denmark with a 2-0 half-time lead in Kazakhstan. However, their hosts turned the tables on them in the closing stages and they lost 3-2.

Denmark regained momentum in the spring campaign with a home victory over Northern Ireland then a 1-1 draw in Slovenia. Last September, October and November brought an impressive run of five successive victories culminating in an all-important 2-1 defeat of Slovenia. Thomas Delaney, whose 2022 FIFA World Cup had been marred by injury, struck the decisive second goal to reward Denmark's best performance with qualification for the finals.

Victory was all the more impressive for being achieved despite the absences of Højlund, captain Simon Kjær and playmaker Christian Eriksen. Denmark and Slovenia had finished level on 22 points, but Denmark took top spot ahead of Slovenia courtesy of a win and a draw in their mutual matches.

Denmark can look back more than a century to their first successful steps in the international arena. They won the Olympic Games football competition in 1906 and

ABOVE: Denmark are back in the finals in pursuit of a victory to emulate their triumph in 1992. They have also been semi-finalists twice.

DENMARK at the UEFA European Championship

1960	Did not qualify
1964	Fourth place
1968	Did not qualify
1972	Did not qualify
1976	Did not qualify
1980	Did not qualify
1984	Semi-finals
1988	Group stage
1992	WINNERS
1996	Group stage
2000	Group stage
2004	Group stage
2008	Did not qualify
2012	Group stage
2016	Did not qualify
2020*	Semi-finals

*2020 finals were played in 2021

COACH

KASPER HJULMAND

Kasper Hjulmand, 52, launched himself into a coaching career after his playing career was ended by a knee injury at 26. His first major appointment was at Lyngby and then he guided Nordsjælland to the 2012 league title. Hjulmand moved to Germany with Mainz in 2014 before he returned to Nordsjælland and then succeeded Age Hareide with the national team in 2020. In 2021 Hjulmand took Denmark to the semi-finals of the pandemic-delayed UEFA EURO before losing after extra time to England at Wembley. Hjulmand's men failed to progress beyond the group stage at the 2022 FIFA World Cup.

KEY PLAYER

RASMUS HØJLUND

POSITION: Forward
CLUB: Manchester United FC (ENGLAND)
AGE: 21
BORN: 4 February 2003, Copenhagen
INTERNATIONAL DEBUT: 22 September 2022 vs Croatia
CAPS: 10 • **GOALS**: 7

Rasmus Højlund has proved to be the most exciting new arrival on the Denmark scene for many years. The Copenhagen-born forward made his national team debut only during the UEFA Nations League in 2022 and did not make his first start until his hat-trick feat against Finland in the EURO qualifiers. He finished the campaign as Denmark's seven-goal leading marksman. In the meantime Højlund had joined Manchester United in the English Premier League for a fee of £64m. He had begun his career with FC København and made rapid progress up the international football ladder. In January 2022 he joined Austria's Sturm Graz but stayed only six months before being sold to Italy's Atalanta. Højlund scored nine goals in 32 Serie A appearances before being sold on to United last August.

were runners-up in 1908 and 1912. Outstanding players included Nils Middelboe, who later played in England for Chelsea.

A subsequent period in the international shadows ended in the 1970s. A flood of outstanding players – led by 1977 European Footballer of the Year Allan Simonsen – left Denmark to play abroad. This prompted an end in 1976 to a ban on 'exiles' playing for the national team. Stars such as Simonsen, Michael Laudrup, Preben Elkjær, Jesper Olsen, Morten Olsen and Søren Lerby brought home their top-level experience and results were dramatic. Suddenly Denmark became a power again on the national team stage.

These players and other new stars formed the nucleus of the side who reached the semi-finals at the 1984 European Championship in France and the round of 16 at the World Cup in Mexico two years later. A new generation, including Michael Laudrup's brother Brian, then propelled Denmark to the European title in 1992. Denmark, remarkably, had been summoned to the finals at very short notice to replace Yugoslavia.

Subsequently Denmark have reached the EURO and World Cup finals on five occasions. The most successful of all these campaigns was three years ago when Denmark reached the semi-finals of the delayed 2020 finals. Captain Kjær and the DBU's medical team received UEFA awards for their swift reaction after playmaker Christian Eriksen suffered a cardiac arrest during a group stage match against Finland.

Eriksen recovered to resume his career at club and national team levels. He is one of nine players in the squad who have more than 50 national appearances to their name.

Kasper Schmeichel has been first-choice goalkeeper for a decade while the defenders in front of him have been led by Kjær, Denmark's record international, alongside Andreas Christensen and Jens Stryger Larsen. Eriksen's supporting cast in midfield has featured Delaney and Pierre-Emile Højbjerg, to help create the attacking openings for Martin Braithwaite and the exciting newcomer Højlund.

DID YOU KNOW?

Denmark will journey to Germany to appear at the UEFA EURO for the tenth time in all and the third in the past four tournaments.

GROUP C
SERBIA

Serbia are heading into the UEFA EURO in their own right for the first time since the fragmentation of the former Yugoslavia. Coach Dragan Stojković's squad emerged from a tense finale to an awkward qualifying group, demonstrating the ability of the players at his disposal.

An image of the original Yugoslavia as the 'Argentina of Europe', because of all its exported football talent, had been generated as far back as 1930. That was when Yugoslavia were one of only four European nations to compete at the inaugural FIFA World Cup in Uruguay. They were pioneers again at the first Nations' Cup in 1958–60. Yugoslavia reached the final in Paris before losing to the Soviet Union.

They were runners-up again in 1968 while Crvena zvezda, one of their two leading clubs along with Partizan, won both the UEFA Cup and then the European Cup before Yugoslavia broke up in the early 1990s. Serbia and Montenegro emerged with a national team that reached the World Cup finals in France in 1998, inspired by stars such as Dejan Savićević, Predrag Mijatović and Siniša Mihajlović.

Two years later Serbia and Montenegro reached the EURO in Belgium and the Netherlands. They progressed to the quarter-finals before losing to their Dutch co-hosts. The political union with Montenegro was dissolved in 2006. Since then Serbia have appeared three times at the World Cup finals, but this will be their first EURO campaign as a stand alone nation.

Serbia were drawn in Group G, which featured neighbouring Bulgaria,

ABOVE: Serbia are ending a two-decade absence from the main stage after finally qualifying for a return to the UEFA EURO finals.

SERBIA
at the UEFA European Championship

1960**	Runners-up
1964**	Did not qualify
1968**	Runners-up
1972**	Did not qualify
1976**	Fourth place
1980**	Did not qualify
1984**	Group stage
1988**	Did not qualify
1992**	Disqualified
1996**	Did not participate
2000**	Quarter-finals
2004***	Did not qualify
2008	Did not qualify
2012	Did not qualify
2016	Did not qualify
2020*	Did not qualify

*2020 finals were played in 2021
**As Yugoslavia / ***As Serbia and Montenegro

COACH

DRAGAN STOJKOVIĆ

Dragan Stojković, 59, was appointed on his birthday in March 2021, just in time to lead Serbia to the FIFA World Cup finals and now to UEFA EURO 2024. 'Piksi' Stojković, nicknamed after a cartoon character, came to the job with the status of being one of Serbia's greatest modern footballers. He scored 15 goals in 84 appearances for the former Yugoslavia, many of them as captain. Later he was president of the national football federation and then of his old club, Crzena zvezda, before coaching in both Japan and China.

KEY PLAYER

DUŠAN TADIĆ

POSITION: Forward
CLUB: Fenerbahçe SK (TÜRKIYE)
AGE: 35
BORN: 20 November 1988, Bačka Topola
INTERNATIONAL DEBUT: 14 December 2008 vs Poland
CAPS: 104 · **GOALS**: 22

Dušan Tadić played for Serbia at the 2008 Beijing Olympic Games and was then promoted into the senior national team for an end-of-year friendly against Poland. He appeared for Serbia at the finals of the FIFA World Cup in 2018 and 2022 when he was team captain in Qatar. Tadić celebrated his 100th international appearance in a 3-1 win in Lithuania during EURO qualifying last September. Tadić's senior club career has taken him from Vojvodina, to the Netherlands with Groningen and Twente, on to England with Southampton and then back to the Netherlands with Ajax. He spent five outstanding years in Amsterdam, winning three Dutch league titles and two domestic cups as well as being hailed as player of the season in 2021. He signed for Fenerbahçe in July last year.

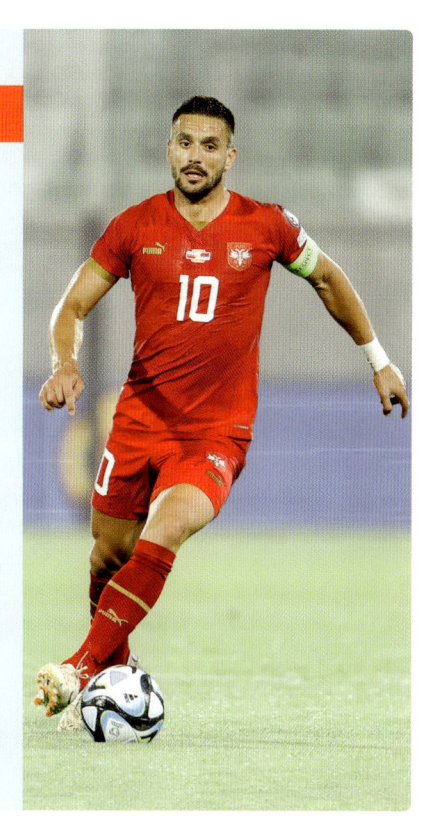

Hungary and Montenegro plus Lithuania, whom they defeated 2-0 in their opening fixture in Belgrade. Veteran Dušan Tadić and Juventus' Dušan Vlahović scored the goals either side of half-time to provide a perfect start. Vlahović followed up with the two late goals which decided the 'derby' away to former partners Montenegro in Podgorica. Serbia thus wound up the spring schedule joint top of the table with Hungary.

The autumn resumption brought defeats both home and away by Hungary before Serbia regained form with a home defeat of Montenegro. Record marksman Aleksandar Mitrović scored twice in a 3-1 win which set up a tense finale at home to Bulgaria.

Serbia kicked off two points ahead of Montenegro and two behind already-qualified Hungary. One point would be enough to guarantee qualification even if Montenegro won in Budapest. The tie hung in the balance as Bulgaria seized a 2-1 lead midway through the second half. Eight minutes of normal time remained when Srđan Babić headed home from close range to secure the draw, the point and qualification in second place.

Veteran coach Dragan Stojković will look once more to Mitrović to provide a constant attacking threat at the finals. Mitrović, a European youth champion with Serbia and Montenegro, has been leading the senior national team attack for a decade and now has a talented partner in Vlahović.

Goalkeeping duties have been shared between Mallorca's Predrag Rajković and Torino's Vanja Milinković-Savić while defensive security has been the charge of Sevilla's Nemanja Gudelj and Fiorentina's Nikola Milinković. Further forward, coach Stojković has been spoiled for choice in midfield by Tadić above all but also Juventus' Filip Kostić, Getafe's Nemanja Maksimović, Panathinaikos' Filip Đuričić, Torino's Nemanja Radonjić and Fulham's Saša Lukić.

It has been a long wait but Serbia are back.

DID YOU KNOW?

Serbian footballers have been absent from the finals since the then Serbia and Montenegro made their tournament debut 24 years ago.

GROUP C
ENGLAND

England bring not only their history but a proven taste for tournament competition into UEFA EURO 2024. They will also be burning with an ambition to take the long-awaited last decisive step to glory after being defeated on penalties by Italy at Wembley in the dramatic climax to the last edition.

Gareth Southgate, after eight years in charge, counts as one of the most experienced national team managers in the game. He knows all about the trials, tribulations and celebrations every tournament has in store. By the end of the qualifying tournament he had managed England on 91 occasions, a tally exceeded only by Sir Bobby Robson (95), Sir Alf Ramsey (113) and Sir Walter Winterbottom (139).

England first made their mark in what was then the Nations' Cup in its third edition in 1968, when the then FIFA World Cup holders reached the semi-finals. The Three Lions did not progress deep into the finals again until reaching the last four as hosts in 1996. Their dreams were shattered in front of their own fans at Wembley by a penalty shoot-out defeat against Germany. Southgate was the unfortunate player to fail with England's last shot.

Southgate's return to duty in 2016, now as manager, saw England reach the semi-finals of both the World Cup in 2018 and UEFA Nations League in 2019. England maintained their high profile by reaching the final of EURO 2020 and then the World Cup quarter-finals in 2022 in Qatar.

The nucleus of Southgate's England team has been a model of consistency. Key figures included

ABOVE: England will be challenging at the finals for the 11th time, having been absent only once since appearing in the group stage in 1988.

ENGLAND at the UEFA European Championship

1960	Did not enter
1964	Did not qualify
1968	Third place
1972	Did not qualify
1976	Did not qualify
1980	Group stage
1984	Did not qualify
1988	Group stage
1992	Group stage
1996	Semi-finals
2000	Group stage
2004	Quarter-finals
2008	Did not qualify
2012	Quarter-finals
2016	Round of 16
2020*	Runners-up

*2020 finals were played in 2021

COACH

GARETH SOUTHGATE

Gareth Southgate boasts a proud record as manager of England, having led his country to the final of UEFA EURO 2020 after reaching the semi-finals of the FIFA World Cup in Russia in 2018. Southgate, aged 53, had played 57 times for England mainly as a defensive midfielder between 1995 and 2004. This meant he saw finals action at the World Cup in 1998 and the EUROs in 1996 and 2000. Later Southgate managed Middlesbrough for three years until 2009 when he joined the Football Association. He managed the Under-21s from 2013 to 2016, when he moved up to senior team manager.

KEY PLAYER

JUDE BELLINGHAM

POSITION: Midfield
CLUB: Real Madrid CF (SPAIN)
AGE: 20
BORN: 29 June 2003, Stourbridge
INTERNATIONAL DEBUT: 2 November 2020 vs Rep of Ireland
CAPS: 27 · **GOALS**: 2

Jude Bellingham has established himself as one of Europe's most exciting young players since graduating from Birmingham City and Borussia Dortmund to Real Madrid last summer for an initial €103m. The attacking midfielder was Birmingham's youngest competitive newcomer on making his debut aged 16 years, 38 days in 2019. He spent three seasons at Dortmund, winning the German Cup and being voted Bundesliga Player of the Season. At Madrid, Bellingham took over the great Zinedine Zidane's No5 shirt and made an explosive start with ten goals in his first ten games. His England career brought progress via the Under-15s, Under-16s, Under-17s and Under-21s before a senior debut in 2020 and appearances at UEFA EURO 2020 and the 2022 FIFA World Cup. In Qatar he scored in England's win over Iran.

Jordan Pickford in goal, Kyle Walker, John Stones and Harry Maguire in defence, Declan Rice in midfield and Harry Kane at the centre of attack, variously supported by Phil Foden, Bukayo Saka, Marcus Rashford and Jack Grealish. The latest plus factor for England in heading to Germany has been the exciting emergence of Jude Bellingham. The Real Madrid midfielder featured in England's squad at EURO 2020 before establishing himself as a starter during the 2022 World Cup and the EURO 2024 qualifiers.

England seized command of qualifying Group C from the outset in March last year. They served notice on the rest of Europe by defeating reigning champions Italy 2-1 in the Stadio Diego Armando Maradona in Naples. When Kane, with a penalty, scored England's second, he exceeded Wayne Rooney's record of 53 goals. England held on for their first win in Italy since 1961 despite a red card in the closing stages for defender Luke Shaw.

Kane and Co followed through with victories at home to Ukraine, away to Malta, home to North Macedonia – in which Saka scored a hat-trick – before dropping their first points in a 1-1 draw with Ukraine in Wroclaw, Poland. This proved merely a temporary setback.

Ultimately qualification was assured next time out by a 3-1 victory over Italy at Wembley. This was England's first home win over the Azzurri since 1977. Kane scored twice, once from a penalty, to extend his England total and exceed Sir Bobby Charlton's record of 23 goals by an England player at Wembley.

England, with two games to spare, had thus secured their ticket for Germany, where Southgate accepted they would be among the favourites. He said, after the Wembley defeat of Italy: "We have to accept the expectations. Pressure comes when expectation is different to reality and the reality is that we are going to be one of the teams capable of winning in Germany. We're comfortable with that."

DID YOU KNOW?

England played their first match, against Scotland, in 1872 but did not play against any non-British or Irish opposition until 1908.

1984

Magic Moments:
PLATINI'S RECORD

27 JUNE 1984 / PARIS

Michel Platini was top-scoring captain as hosts France succeeded 1980 winners West Germany to become champions of Europe. Victory made amends for the hosts' semi-final defeat in front of their own fans in 1960. Coach Michel Hidalgo's France built success on the foundation of a skilled midfield in which Platini was supported by Alain Giresse, Jean Tigana and Luis Fernández. The group stage saw Platini strike a lone winner in the opening match against Denmark then hat-tricks against Belgium and Yugoslavia. Then his late extra-time goal edged Portugal in a thrilling semi-final. Platini crowned a perfect tournament by converting a free kick for the first goal in a 2-0 victory over Spain in the final after which, as captain, he raised aloft the Henri Delaunay Cup.

RIGHT: Top-scoring captain Michel Platini converts a free kick to open the scoring for France in their defeat of Spain in the 1984 final.

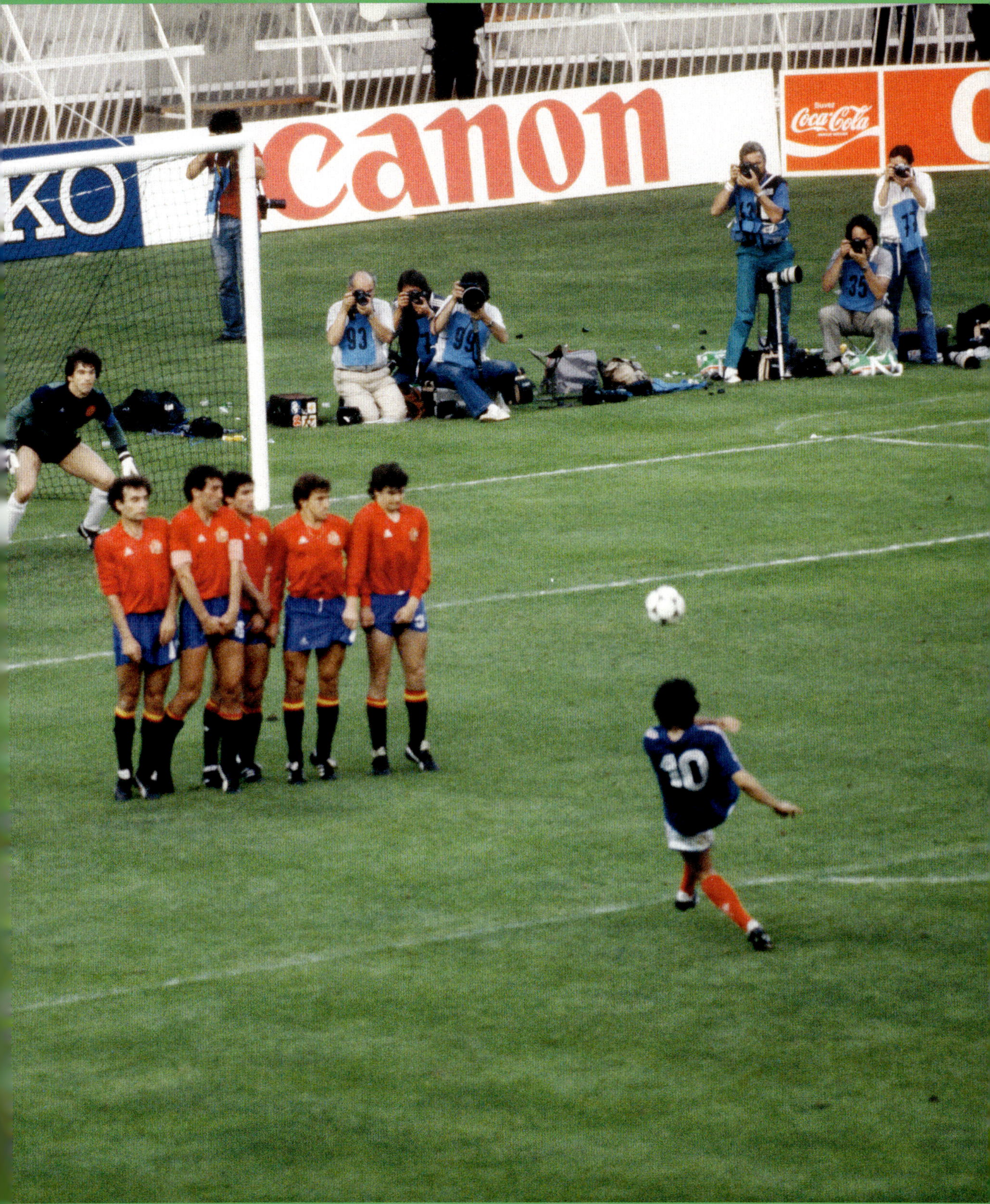
KO
canon
Coca-Cola

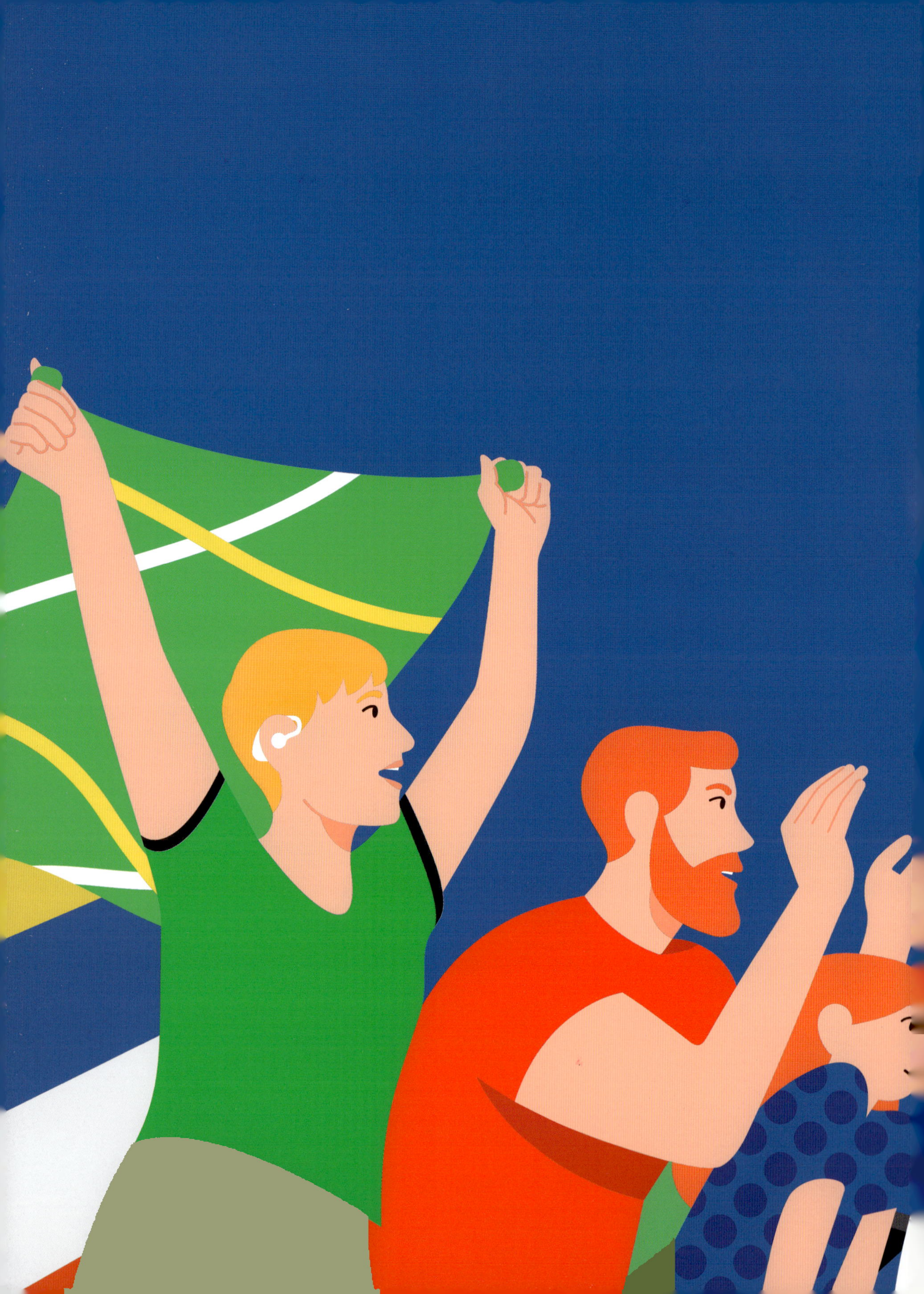

UEFA EURO 2024 GERMANY

GROUP D

France have been champions twice, runners-up once and semi-finalists twice. The Netherlands were champions in 1988 and semi-finalists four times. Both France and the Netherlands reached the round of 16 at UEFA EURO 2020. Austria also reached the round of 16 at EURO 2020 in only their third appearance at the finals.

- Play-off Winner A
- Netherlands
- Austria
- France

Play-offs: Path A
POLAND

Poland, having reached the round of 16 at the FIFA World Cup in Qatar in 2022, then finished third in Group E of the UEFA EURO 2024 qualifying competition.

Finishing behind Albania and Czechia was a disappointment for the Polish Football Association and the team's fans. Their failure to qualify directly led to the departure of Poland's veteran Portuguese coach Fernando Santos and the appointment of Michał Probierz, who had been overseeing the Under-21s in their own UEFA championship. Poland's most important player remained their captain, Robert Lewandowski, who has been voted Poland's footballer of the year a record 11 times, won the Golden Shoe as Europe's leading league marksman in 2021 and 2022 and has twice been hailed as FIFA's best men's player. He played previously for Legia Warsaw, Znicz Pruszków and Lech Poznań, then in Germany with Borussia Dortmund and Bayern München. Poland's other most experienced players in the EURO campaign included goalkeeper Wojciech Szczęsny, defenders Bartosz Bereszyński and Jan Bednarek, midfielders Grzegorz Krychowiak and Kamil Grosicki, plus forward Arkadiusz Milik.

COACH
MICHAŁ PROBIERZ

KEY PLAYER
ROBERT LEWANDOWSKI
POSITION: Forward
CLUB: FC Barcelona (SPAIN)
AGE: 35

Poland reached the play-offs via their UEFA Nations League A placing.

Play-offs: Path A
WALES

Wales entered the play-offs chasing a third successive appearance at the finals after reaching the last four in 2016 and then the round of 16 at UEFA EURO 2020.

Coach Robert Page and his Red Dragons missed out on direct qualification after finishing third in Group D behind Türkiye and Croatia. They entered the play-offs through the UEFA Nations League. Wales were well placed for a dramatic finish in their EURO qualifying group, but dropped out of the reckoning after being held to 1-1 draws in their last matches against Armenia and Türkiye. Their attack now missed the leadership of record marksman Gareth Bale, who had retired after the FIFA World Cup in Qatar, where Wales did not progress beyond the group stage. Page still possessed a squad with competitive experience in goalkeeper Wayne Hennessey, defenders Ben Davies and Connor Roberts, midfielders Harry Wilson and Ethan Ampadu, plus exciting winger Daniel James and the up-and-coming Tottenham forward Brennan Johnson. Above all, Wales could still call on the skill of Aaron Ramsey in midfield. Ramsey was now back in Wales with Cardiff after spells with Arsenal, Nottingham Forest, Juventus, Rangers and Nice.

COACH
ROBERT PAGE

KEY PLAYER
AARON RAMSEY
POSITION: Midfielder
CLUB: Cardiff City FC (WALES)
AGE: 33

Wales were semi-finalists at UEFA EURO 2016 in France.

Play-offs: Path A
FINLAND

COACH
MARKKU KANERVA

KEY PLAYER
DANIEL HÅKANS
POSITION: Forward
CLUB: Vålerenga Fotball (FINLAND)
AGE: 23

Finland's ambition in contesting the play-offs is a return to the finals after making their debut on the major international stage at UEFA EURO 2020.

Coach Markku Kanerva, a former schoolteacher who was appointed in 2016, led Finland to third place in a tightly contested EURO qualifying Group H behind Denmark and Slovenia. They progressed to the play-offs after having finished second in Group B3 of UEFA Nations League B behind Bosnia and Herzegovina. Finland's top scorer in the EURO qualifying campaign was Daniel Håkans, a 23-year-old winger from Vålerenga. Having made his national team debut only midway through the qualifying campaign in June 2023, he then marked his second appearance by scoring three goals in nine minutes as a second-half substitute in a 6-0 win over San Marino. Finland's attack also benefited from the widely travelled experience of Teemu Pukki, who is the country's all-time top scorer with more than 30 goals in his 100-plus appearances since 2009. Pukki is now playing his football in the United States with Minnesota United, whom he joined last year after five years in English league football with Norwich City.

Finland are targeting a second successive EURO final tournament campaign.

Play-offs: Path A
ESTONIA

COACH
THOMAS HÄBERLI

KEY PLAYER
KAROL METS
POSITION: Defender
CLUB: FC St Pauli (GERMANY)
AGE: 30

Estonia entered the play-offs within tantalising sight of achieving a place among Europe's competitive elite for the first time in their football history.

Estonia began playing international football in 1920, but a 50-year hiatus followed after the country's annexation by the Soviet Union. Estonia regained its independence at the start of the 1990s and witnessed its first formal international match of a brand new era with a 1-1 draw against Slovenia in Tallinn in 1992. Until now, they have never progressed beyond the qualifying stages of either the FIFA World Cup or the UEFA European Championship. This time around, despite finishing bottom of their EURO 2024 qualfiying group, Estonia secured a second bite of the cherry via the UEFA Nations League, winning all four of their matches in Group D2, scoring ten goals and conceding just two. Those Nations League wins came in home-and-away match-ups against Malta and San Marino, and also mean they will be playing in UEFA Nations League C in the next edition of the competition. Estonia's head coach since January 2021 has been the 49-year-old former Switzerland forward Thomas Häberli.

Estonia have never reached a EURO final tournament.

GROUP D
NETHERLANDS

Dutch football has been thrilling the international game for five decades. The legacy of the total football revolution initiated by Johan Cruyff continues to inspire at both national team and club levels. Yet the Oranje's only major prize remains the European crown back in 1988. Time to change all that.

As the Netherlands prepare to return to Germany, where they triumphed at the UEFA European Championship 36 years ago, captain Virgil van Dijk is confident about the team's chances: "I think we can be proud of ourselves despite the injuries we had. We fought well as a team and can build on that. Then it can be a great European Championship."

The Netherlands reached the final tournament as runners-up to France in qualifying Group B. The high-profile duel between two nations edged out by Argentina during the climactic stages of the FIFA World Cup in December 2022 was very much in evidence right from the start of EURO 2024 qualifying. The Netherlands, under new coach Ronald Koeman, lost 4-0 at the Stade de France but pulled their campaign back on track three days later when two goals from Nathan Aké delivered a 3-0 home win over Gibraltar.

The Netherlands returned to qualifying action in the autumn with another 3-0 victory, over Greece. Cody Gakpo was on the scoresheet and then again in a hard-earned 2-1 win away to the Republic of Ireland in Dublin. A narrow home defeat by France was followed by victories over Greece and the Republic of Ireland, which delivered qualification with one game to spare. Wout Weghorst scored the all-important goal.

ABOVE: The Netherlands have competed in ten UEFA EUROs, being crowned European champions in 1988 and reaching the semi-finals four other times.

NETHERLANDS at the UEFA European Championship

1960	Did not enter
1964	Did not qualify
1968	Did not qualify
1972	Did not qualify
1976	Third place
1980	Group stage
1984	Did not qualify
1988	WINNERS
1992	Semi-finals
1996	Quarter-finals
2000	Semi-finals
2004	Semi-finals
2008	Quarter-finals
2012	Group stage
2016	Did not qualify
2020*	Round of 16

*2020 finals were played in 2021

COACH

RONALD KOEMAN

Ronald Koeman was an outstanding defender whose ferocious shot earned 14 goals in 78 games for the Netherlands between 1982 and 1994. His national team highlight was winning the 1988 European Championship alongside 18 major club honours with Ajax, PSV Eindhoven and Barcelona. Koeman coached numerous European club sides, including Ajax, PSV, Benfica and Valencia, before taking up an initial appointment with the Dutch national team, whom he guided to the runners-up spot in the 2018/19 UEFA Nations League. Subsequently, Koeman returned to club football with Barcelona before being reappointed last year, succeeding Louis van Gaal after the FIFA World Cup.

KEY PLAYER

CODY GAKPO

POSITION: Forward
CLUB: Liverpool FC (ENGLAND)
AGE: 25
BORN: 7 May 1999, Eindhoven
INTERNATIONAL DEBUT: 21 June 2021 vs North Macedonia
CAPS: 21 • **GOALS**: 9

Cody Gakpo earned special status for himself at UEFA EURO 2020 as one of the handful of players who have made their national team debut during a EURO final tournament. Gakpo, then with PSV Eindhoven, has gone from strength to strength, winning the Dutch footballer of the year award in 2022, before starring at the World Cup finals in Qatar. In January 2023, he moved to the English Premier League, joining Liverpool for £37m. Gakpo could have chosen to play for Togo, his father's birthplace, but had no hesitation as a teenager in representing the Netherlands at Under-18, Under-19, Under-20 and Under-21 levels. He made his senior debut as a substitute against North Macedonia at EURO 2020.

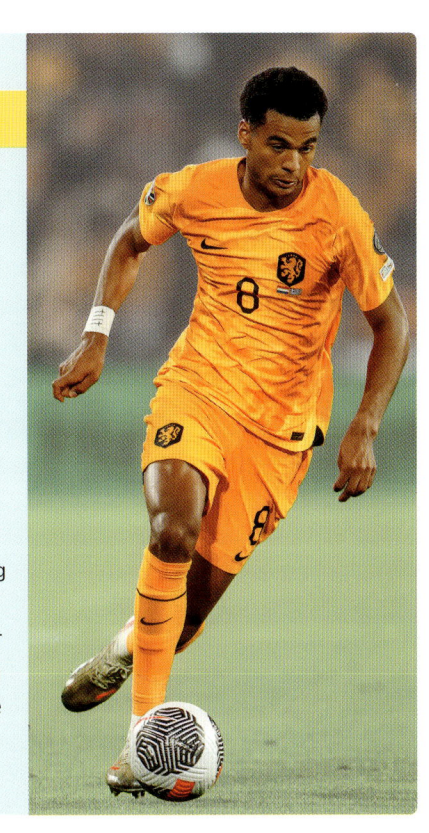

After reaching the round of 16 at the delayed UEFA EURO 2020 and the quarter-finals of the FIFA World Cup in December 2022, both under their previous head coach Louis van Gaal, the Netherlands will be looking to go even further at this summer's EURO.

The Netherlands were among the continent's leading teams in the early 1900s. They reached the semi-finals of four consecutive Olympic Games from 1908 to 1924 and won the bronze medal twice. A modernisation of the domestic game in the mid-1950s brought the introduction of professionalism and dramatic success both at home and abroad for Ajax, Feyenoord and PSV Eindhoven.

The late 1960s and early 1970s saw coach Rinus Michels mastermind the total football explosion. Cruyff, one of the greatest of modern footballers, led record champions Ajax to three successive triumphs in the European Champion Clubs' Cup, while the national team were runners-up both at the 1974 World Cup in West Germany and the 1978 World Cup in Argentina. A further generation in the 1980s brought yet more European success. Ruud Gullit, Marco van Basten, Frank Rijkaard and current coach Ronald Koeman led the national team to victory at the 1988 European Championship in West Germany. The Netherlands went on to reach the semi-finals of the 1998 World Cup, EURO 2000, which they co-hosted with neighbours Belgium, and then EURO 2004 in Portugal.

The Netherlands' squad for the EURO 2024 qualifying campaign boasted enormous experience at the back, led by Van Dijk alongside Aké, Stefan de Vrij, Matthijs de Ligt and Daley Blind, who has been a pillar of the team's defence since 2013. The experience of Italy-based Marten de Roon from Atalanta and Barcelona's Frenkie de Jong in the engine room was also an important factor in allowing versatile wingback Denzel Dumfries to spring from defence and support the dangerous Gakpo and Memphis Depay in attack.

Both Dumfries and Gakpo were outstanding in their team's run to the quarter-finals of the World Cup in Qatar, while Atlético de Madrid's Depay has scored at a rate of one goal every two games for his country.

DID YOU KNOW?

UEFA EURO 2024 will be the Netherlands' 11th EURO final tournament. They qualified first in 1976 and have missed out only twice since then.

GROUP D
AUSTRIA

Austria have secured their status at the top table of the European national team game yet again after failing to qualify for the first 12 tournaments — a span of almost 50 years. An important springboard proved to be Austria's highly praised co-hosting of UEFA EURO 2008.

Just as four years ago, Austria secured their place in the finals as runners-up in their qualifying group. Ahead of the pan-European EURO 2020 tournament they were second to group winners Poland. This time around they pushed qualifying Group F leaders Belgium all the way to Germany and finished decisively clear of Sweden, Azerbaijan and Estonia.

New national coach Ralf Rangnick made his presence felt during qualifying, seeing his men cruise to an opening 4-1 victory over Azerbaijan. Subsequently they extended their winning form in three of their next four games. The odd result out was a creditable 1-1 draw away to Belgium's Red Devils in Brussels courtesy of a first-half own goal by Orel Mangala.

The Belgians then turned the tables on Austria by winning 3-2 in Vienna; late goals from Konrad Laimer and Marcel Sabitzer set up a dramatic finish in vain. Ultimately that defeat barely mattered. The Austrians secured their spot in the finals next time out by completing a second victory over Azerbaijan. Austria's leading scorer, attacking midfielder Sabitzer, struck the lone winning goal from the penalty spot early in the second half at the Tofig Bahramov Stadium in Baku.

Austria command a historic role in European football. In 1902 they

ABOVE: Austria have competed in every competition since its creation in 1958-60, but did not make a finals debut until their co-hosting with Switzerland in 2008.

AUSTRIA
at the UEFA European Championship

1960	Did not qualify
1964	Did not qualify
1968	Did not qualify
1972	Did not qualify
1976	Did not qualify
1980	Did not qualify
1984	Did not qualify
1988	Did not qualify
1992	Did not qualify
1996	Did not qualify
2000	Did not qualify
2004	Did not qualify
2008	Group stage
2012	Did not qualify
2016	Group stage
2020*	Round of 16

*2020 finals were played in 2021

COACH

RALF RANGNICK

Ralf Rangnick took over the role of Austria boss in 2022, the first national team appointment of his 40-year managerial career. Rangnick, 65, spent his playing career in the lower divisions before turning to coaching aged 25. He built his reputation with VfB Stuttgart, Hannover 96 and Schalke before lifting Hoffenheim into the Bundesliga and winning the German Cup back with Schalke. Next, Rangnick masterminded RB Leipzig's rise before spells with Lokomotiv Moscow and Manchester United. He has been hailed as a major influence on a generation of leading German coaches..

KEY PLAYER

MARCEL SABITZER

POSITION: Midfield
CLUB: Borussia Dortmund (GERMANY)
AGE: 29
BORN: 17 March 1994, Weis
INTERNATIONAL DEBUT: 5 June 2012 vs Romania
CAPS: 75 · **GOALS**: 16

Marcel Sabitzer brings added value to both Austria and all the clubs for whom he has played. Sabitzer can play in every midfield role or in attacking support and has a sharp eye for goal. One of his goals, a second-half penalty, brought Austria the 1-0 victory over Azerbaijan to seal their place at UEFA EURO 2024. Sabitzer played for Admira Wacker, Rapid and Salzburg before moving to Germany with RB Leipzig. He had a spell on loan in the English Premier League with Manchester United before returning to the Bundesliga with Borussia Dortmund.

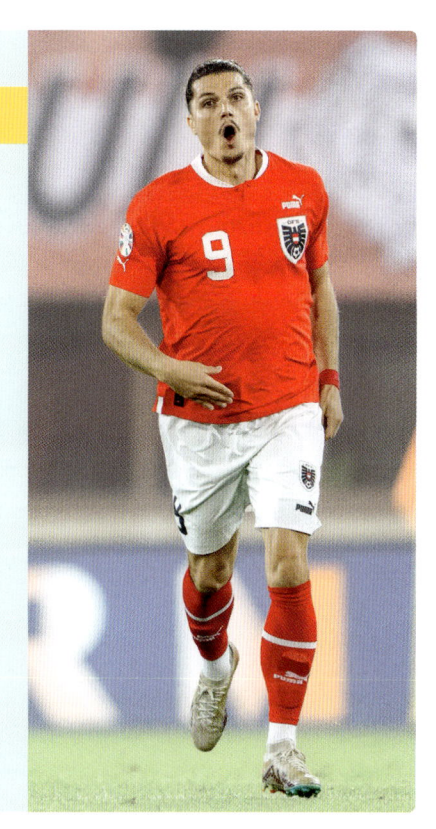

beat Hungary 5-0 in Vienna in what stands as the world's second oldest regular international fixture after England vs Scotland.

A crucial factor in the development of Austrian football was the pioneering work of Hugo Meisl, the federation's general secretary and also national team manager. Meisl took a leading role in helping to found the European International Cup of Nations, an inter-war central European forerunner of UEFA's continental championship. Austria were winners once and runners-up once in the era of the legendary *Wunderteam*, led by Mathias Sindelar, the iconic 'Man of Paper'. They were also semi-finalists at the FIFA World Cup in 1934.

Inspirational players in the 1950s were half-backs Ernst Ocwirk and Gerhard Hanappi, but a decline set in after Austria hit a post-war high point on reaching the semi-finals of the 1954 World Cup. The depression deepened in 1991 after a 1-0 qualifying defeat by EURO newcomers Faroe Islands.

The road back to the international high table has been rocky. Since then Austria have appeared in the group stage of the FIFA World Cup only once but in the EUROs three times. At EURO 2020 the Austrians reached the round of 16 before losing to eventual champions Italy 2-1 after extra time.

Franco Foda was succeeded as team manager by fellow German Ralf Rangnick in the wake of Austria's failure to reach the finals of the World Cup in Qatar in 2022. Rangnick has refreshed the squad extensively from the selection called up for the last EURO.

Survivors from 2021 in the latest qualifying series included goalkeeper Alexander Schlager; defenders David Alaba and Philipp Lienhart; midfielders Christoph Baumgartner, Laimer and Xaver Schlager; plus forwards Saša Kalajdžić, Michael Gregoritsch, Marko Arnautović and – most importantly – Sabitzer.

Austria, relying on a squad drawn largely from clubs in the domestic championship and in Germany, are ready to compete at the top level again.

DID YOU KNOW?

Austria's legendary *Wunderteam* of the late 1920s and 1930s owed their winning style to an English coach, Jimmy Hogan, who introduced them to the Scottish passing game.

GROUP D
FRANCE

France have a unique relationship with this competition. The trophy is named after Frenchman Henri Delaunay, who was a leading light in the tournament's creation, and France hosted the first finals in 1960. Champions in both 1984 and 2000, they hope to emulate Germany and Spain as triple winners.

Evolution rather than revolution has served France well under the management of Didier Deschamps. He is one of only three men, along with Brazil's Mário Zagallo and Germany's Franz Beckenbauer, to have both captained and managed their countries to success in the men's World Cup. However, the EURO double has so far eluded Deschamps. He captained France to victory in 2000 but had to settle for being a runner-up as manager in 2016.

Deschamps is the latest in a long sequence of significant French influencers in international football. Robert Guerin and Jules Rimet built up FIFA ahead of the inaugural World Cup while Delaunay and player-turned-journalist Gabriel Hanot were instrumental in devising European international team and club competitions.

French pride is vested not only in administration but out on the pitch. Lucien Laurent scored the very first goal in the inaugural FIFA World Cup while Michel Platini holds the EURO record of nine goals in one finals tournament when France won the European title for the first time, as hosts, in 1984.

Platini inherited the French superstar crown of 1950s' hero Raymond Kopa and would be followed in turn by Zinedine Zidane, a team-

ABOVE: France, champions in 1984 and 2000, are competing in the finals for the 11th time, placing them fourth in the overall appearance standings.

FRANCE at the UEFA European Championship

1960	Fourth place
1964	Did not qualify
1968	Did not qualify
1972	Did not qualify
1976	Did not qualify
1980	Did not qualify
1984	WINNERS
1988	Did not qualify
1992	Group stage
1996	Semi-finals
2000	WINNERS
2004	Quarter-finals
2008	Group stage
2012	Quarter-finals
2016	Runners-up
2020*	Round of 16

*2020 finals were played in 2021

COACH

DIDIER DESCHAMPS

Didier Deschamps has experienced the fine line between success and failure at football's highest levels. He led France to glory as captain at the FIFA World Cup in 1998 and as coach in 2018 while also having captained Les Bleus to victory at EURO 2000. Deschamps, 55, later became a runner-up as coach at EURO 2016 and the 2022 World Cup. Deschamps made 103 appearances for France during a 16-year club career with Nantes, Marseille, Bordeaux, Juventus, Chelsea and Valencia. He was appointed national coach in succession to former team-mate Laurent Blanc in 2012.

KEY PLAYER

OLIVIER GIROUD

POSITION: Forward
CLUB: AC Milan (ITALY)
AGE: 37
BORN: 30 September 1986, Chambéry
INTERNATIONAL DEBUT: 11 November 2011 vs United States
CAPS: 128 • **GOALS**: 56

Olivier Giroud wrote his own page in football history at the 2022 FIFA World Cup in Qatar when he overtook the 51-goal record of Thierry Henry to become France's all-time leading scorer. His four goals at the finals for the runners-up also earned him the bronze boot. Giroud, a World Cup winner with France in Russia in 2018, also earned eight major honours at club level with Montpellier, Arsenal, Chelsea and Milan, whom he joined in 2021. These included the UEFA Europa League in 2019 and Champions League in 2021, both with Chelsea. Giroud had never played for France at youth level before being summoned for his senior debut in 2011. He scored the first of his record-breaking goals tally three months later in a 2-1 win over Germany.

mate of Deschamps when France were hailed as world champions in 1998 and European champions two years later. Deschamps then stepped up to manage France to victories in the FIFA World Cup in 2018 and UEFA Nations League in 2021. Their EURO dream that year was ended by Switzerland in the round of 16 in a penalty shoot-out, the same fate which befell them against Argentina in the 2022 World Cup final.

France have moved forward with a team mixing experience and youth and all topped off by the explosive attacking brilliance of captain Kylian Mbappé. Alphonse Areola and Mike Maignan have been competing to succeed the retired Hugo Lloris in goal behind defenders Benjamin Pavard, the Hernández brothers (Lucas and Theo) and Ibrahima Konaté. Real Madrid youngsters Aurélien Tchouaméni and Eduardo Camavinga have injected new energy into midfield while veterans Olivier Giroud and Antoine Griezmann are complemented up front by the younger Kingsley Coman, Ousmane Dembélé, Marcus Thuram and Randal Kolo Muani.

France were drawn in a challenging qualifying Group C which included the Netherlands, Greece and the Republic of Ireland. They responded by conjuring a perfect start to the campaign with a 4-0 victory over the Dutch on home turf at the Stade de France with two-goal Mbappé leading by example. Pavard scored the lone winner against awkward Irish opposition in Dublin before Mbappé took command again with a goal in the victory in Gibraltar and then the decisive penalty which beat Greece.

The Irish were also beaten at the Stade de France, allowing Les Bleus to secure qualification with a tense 2-1 win over the Netherlands in Amsterdam. Mbappé volleyed home in only the seventh minute to end a run of four competitive outings without a goal. Early in the second half he claimed a 42nd international goal which lifted him past Platini into fourth place on the national team's all-time top scorers list.

Newcomer Quilindschy Hartman pulled back one late goal for the hosts but France then clung on tenaciously to secure their ticket for Germany with two matches still to play.

DID YOU KNOW?

France are the only team to have won the quadruple of FIFA World Cup, EURO, UEFA Nations League and FIFA Confederations Cup.

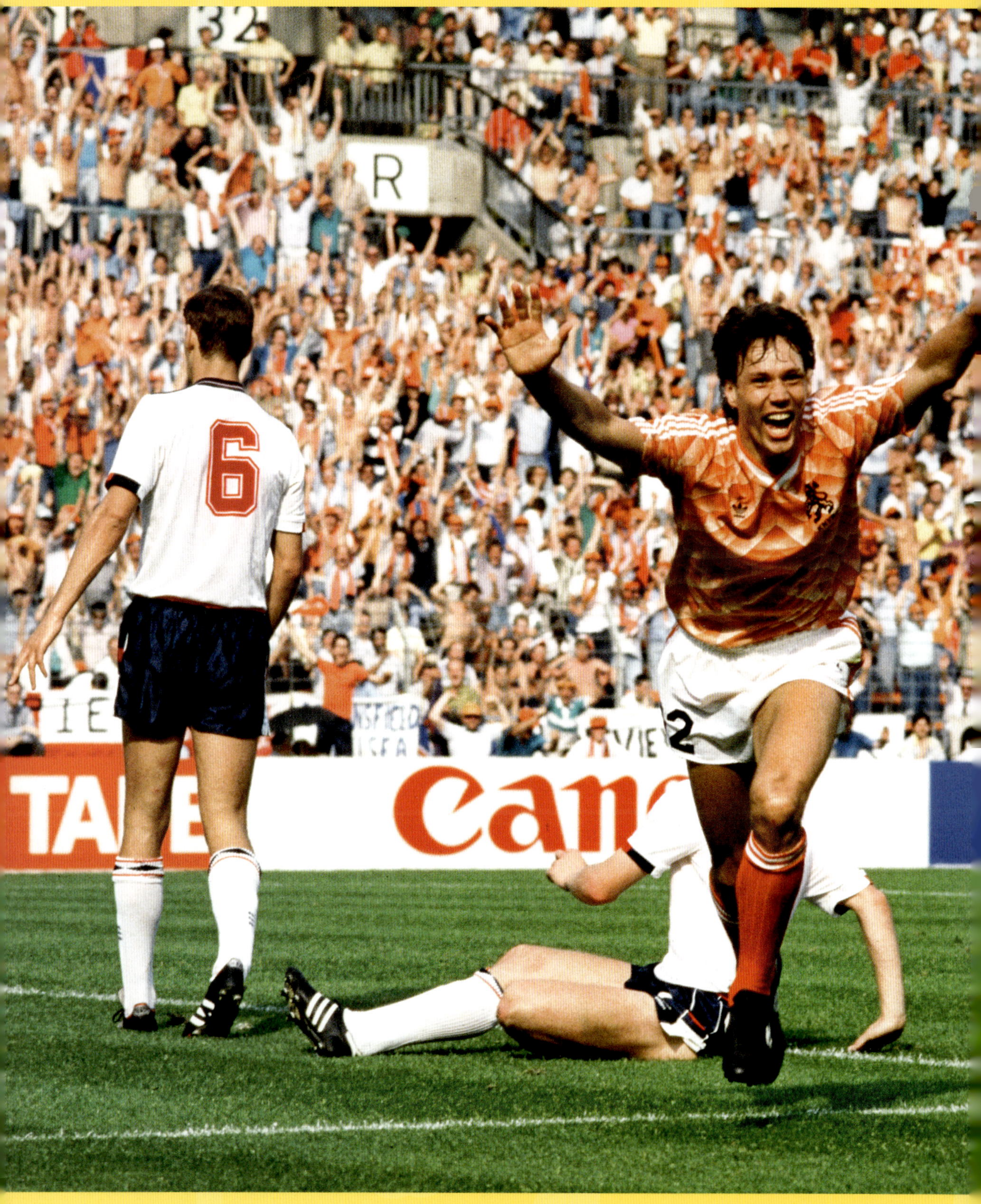
32
R
6

1988

Magic Moments:
DUTCH DELIGHT

15 JUNE 1988 / DÜSSELDORF

The Netherlands achieved a long-overdue international success when they lifted the trophy in 1988. But their campaign got off to the worst of starts in West Germany with a 1-0 defeat by the Soviet Union in their opening group game in Cologne. That prompted coach Rinus Michels into a decisive change for their next clash, against England in Düsseldorf. Michels recalled Marco van Basten to the starting line-up after the Milan forward had been only a late substitute against the USSR. Van Basten made his presence felt in the most explosive manner by scoring all the Netherlands' goals in a 3-1 win. He followed up with the semi-final winner against West Germany and another – an iconic volley from an almost impossible angle – as the revived Dutchmen avenged their opening upset by defeating the Soviet Union 2-0 in the final.

LEFT: Marco van Basten celebrates after striking the first of his three goals for the Netherlands against England in the 1988 group stage in Düsseldorf.

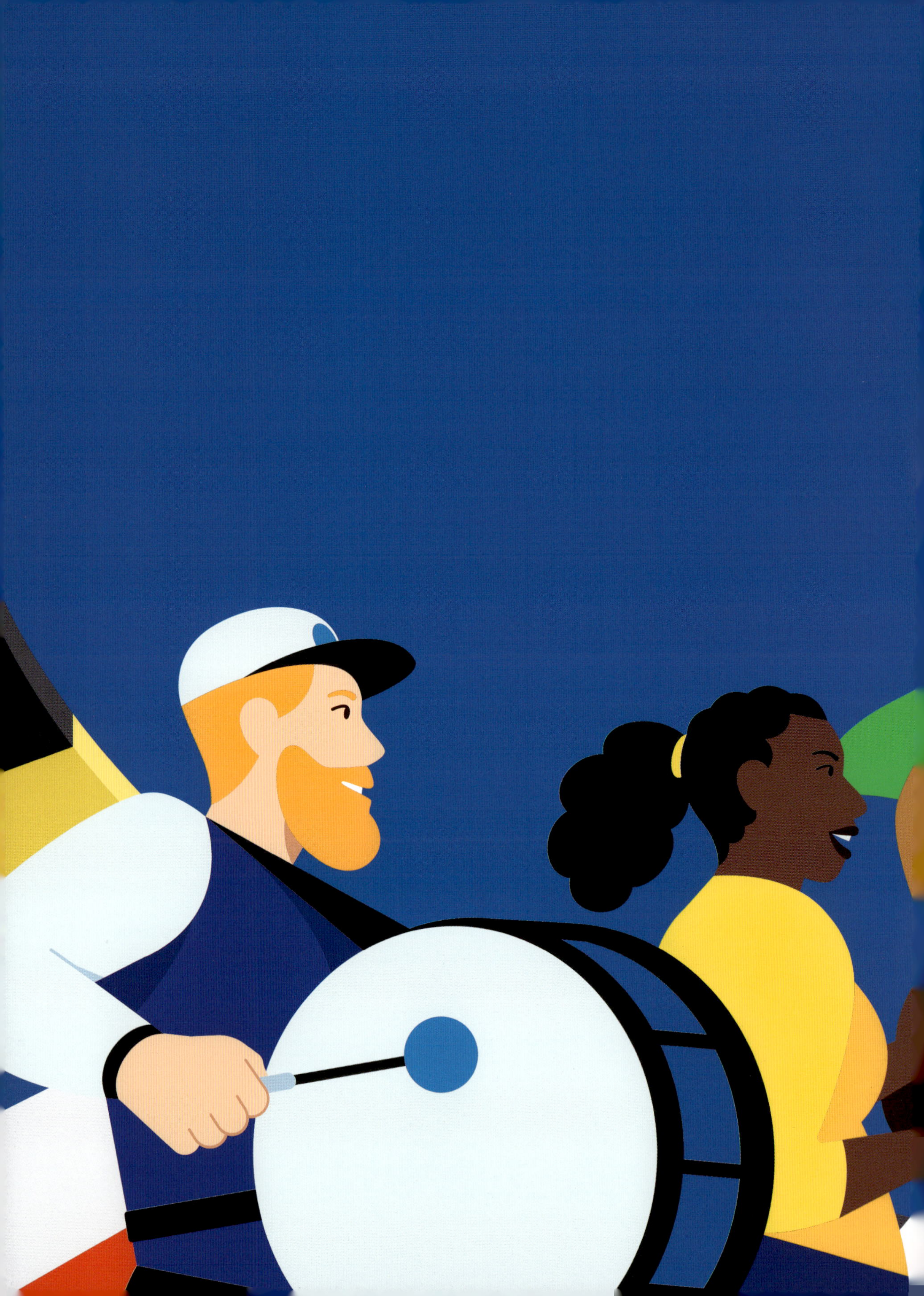

GROUP E

Belgium were runners-up in 1980 after finishing third as hosts in 1972. They were also quarter-finalists on two occasions, including at UEFA EURO 2020. Romania were quarter-finalists in 2000. Slovakia reached the quarter-finals on their debut in 2016.

- Belgium
- Slovakia
- Romania
- Play-off Winner B

GROUP E
BELGIUM

Belgium have established themselves as one of the powerhouses of European international football, ever-present at the finals of all the major tournaments over the past decade and providing outstanding footballers for major clubs in all the big five leagues.

All that remains is for the Red Devils to land one of the top prizes. UEFA EURO 2024, staged next door in Germany, provides an ideal opportunity for a rebuilt team to erase memories of a disappointingly early exit from the FIFA World Cup in the group stage in Qatar in 2022.

The first step forward was the appointment of Domenico Tedesco as new national coach in the spring of 2023. He had little more than a month to plan his EURO qualifying campaign before Belgium were scheduled to kick off their bid for a third consecutive appearance at the finals with a difficult visit to Sweden.

Toby Alderweireld, Eden Hazard and Simon Mignolet had all retired from international football, so Tedesco named in his line-up only five of the men who had started Belgium's last World Cup tie: goalkeeper Thibaud Courtois, defenders Jan Vertonghen and Timothy Castagne, midfielders Kevin De Bruyne and Yannick Carrasco, plus forward Leandro Trossard. Romelu Lukaku rose to the challenge in style. He scored three goals to deliver a 3-0 victory which resounded around Europe.

Lukaku scored again in the following 1-1 home draw against Austria and then two more in

ABOVE: Belgium are appearing in the finals for the seventh time, having taken third place as hosts in 1972 and then finishing as runners-up in 1980.

BELGIUM
at the UEFA European Championship

1960	Did not enter
1964	Did not qualify
1968	Did not qualify
1972	Third place
1976	Did not qualify
1980	Runners-up
1984	Group stage
1988	Did not qualify
1992	Did not qualify
1996	Did not qualify
2000	Group stage
2004	Did not qualify
2008	Did not qualify
2012	Did not qualify
2016	Quarter-finals
2020*	Quarter-finals

*2020 finals were played in 2021

COACH

DOMENICO TEDESCO

Domenico Tedesco was appointed in the spring of 2023 to succeed Roberto Martínez after Belgium's group stage exit at the FIFA World Cup. Tedesco, 38, who holds dual Italian-German citizenship, worked with VfB Stuttgart and Hoffenheim before guiding Schalke to second place in the Bundesliga in 2018 and into the UEFA Champions League. Next came a spell with Spartak Moskva before Tedesco returned to Germany with RB Leipzig. In 2022 he led Leipzig to the semi-finals of the UEFA Europa League while also guiding them to success in the German Cup, where they beat Freiburg on penalties.

KEY PLAYER

ROMELU LUKAKU

POSITION: Forward
CLUB: AS Roma (ITALY)
AGE: 30
BORN: 13 May 1993, Antwerp
INTERNATIONAL DEBUT: 3 March 2010 vs Croatia
CAPS: 113 • **GOALS**: 83

Romelu Lukaku is Belgium's all-time leading marksman with more than twice as many goals as the second-placed Eden Hazard (33). His father Roger had played international football for Zaire (now DR Congo). Lukaku was born in Antwerp, began with Lierse then launched his record-breaking top-level career with Anderlecht. Subsequently he took his hunger for goals to England with Chelsea (two spells), West Bromwich Albion, Everton and Manchester United as well as in Italy with Internazionale (twice) and Roma. Lukaku's trophy haul includes the Belgian league, FIFA Club World Cup as well as Italy's Serie A and Coppa Italia. His goals helped lead Belgium to third place at the 2018 FIFA World Cup in Russia, where he scored four goals and provided one assist to win the bronze boot.

victory away to Estonia. Carrasco was the match winner in Azerbaijan before Lukaku resumed normal service. He struck twice in a 5-0 repeat win over Estonia and then one more in the impressive 3-2 victory over Austria in Vienna, which assured Belgium of a place in the finals.

Talented young newcomers such as defensive midfielder Amadou Onana and wingers Jeremy Doku and Johan Bakayoko were now forcing their way into Tedesco's squad. They were offering promise for not only the tests to come at the EURO but hopes for a new "golden generation".

The Belgian FA, founded in 1895, was one of the driving forces behind the formation of world federation FIFA and one of only four European nations to go to Uruguay for the first World Cup in 1930. A major step forward was achieved with the adoption of professionalism in the early 1970s and Belgium finished third at the 1972 European Championship. At the same time, Belgian club sides earned new respect as Anderlecht won the UEFA Cup Winners' Cup and Super Cup twice each in the 1970s and UEFA Cup in 1983. Club Brugge reached the European Cup final in 1978.

In Italy in 1980 a team coached by Guy Thys reached the final in Rome before losing 2-1 to West Germany following a last-minute goal from Horst Hrubesch. Six years later Belgium were World Cup semi-finalists in Mexico.

In 2000 Belgium made history, with the Netherlands, in staging the first co-hosted EURO. They were eliminated in the group stage and then had to wait 16 years before returning to the finals and reaching the last eight in France. Belgium progressed to a third-place finish at the World Cup in Russia then the quarter-finals of EURO 2020. They also spent three years on top of the men's FIFA World Ranking before the 2022 World Cup. Qatar signalled the end of one era so now the EURO in Germany can herald the beginning of a new one.

DID YOU KNOW?

Belgium's Red Devils are the only national team to have led the FIFA World Ranking without ever having won a World Cup or EURO.

GROUP E
SLOVAKIA

Slovakia has been a nation in its own right for only three decades, but the national team have certainly shown their strength in that time. UEFA EURO 2024 marks their third consecutive final-tournament appearance.

The draw for the qualifying competition delivered a busy schedule for a six-team Group J, including former European champions Portugal as well as Bosnia and Herzegovina, Iceland, Liechtenstein and Luxembourg. Portugal, quarter-finalists at the recent 2022 FIFA World Cup in Qatar and with all their attacking talent, were the obvious favourites, so the challenge was targeting the runners-up slot, which would guarantee a place in Germany.

Slovakia kicked off with a disappointing goalless home draw against Luxembourg. Coach Francesco Calzona's men made amends, however, by winning all of their remaining three games in the spring schedule, at home to Bosnia and Herzegovina and away to Iceland and Liechtenstein.

The autumn resumption brought setbacks with a victory over Liechtenstein sandwiched between home and away defeats by Portugal. Slovakia then recovered with a 1-0 win in Luxembourg before hosting Iceland in Bratislava with qualification in sight.

Fans suffered an early scare when Orri Óskarsson headed Iceland in front after 17 minutes, but the hosts dominated the rest of the match. Juraj Kucka equalised on the half-hour and a penalty converted by Ondrej Duda provided a 2-1 half-time lead. Lukáš Haraslín struck twice in the first ten minutes of the second half. Iceland

ABOVE: Slovakia qualified for the last two EUROs and made it as far as the round of 16 at EURO 2016.

SLOVAKIA at the UEFA European Championship

1960**	Third place
1964**	Did not qualify
1968**	Did not qualify
1972**	Did not qualify
1976**	WINNERS
1980**	Third place
1984**	Did not qualify
1988**	Did not qualify
1992**	Did not qualify
1996	Did not qualify
2000	Did not qualify
2004	Did not qualify
2008	Did not qualify
2012	Did not qualify
2016	Round of 16
2020*	Group stage

*2020 finals were played in 2021
**1960–92 as Czechoslovakia

COACH

FRANCESCO CALZONA

Italian Francesco Calzona enjoyed a low-key playing career in the lower divisions in Italy before turning to coaching. He worked as assistant coach to Maurizio Sarri at Perugia, Alessandria, Sorrento, Empoli and Napoli between 2015 and 2018. Calzona stayed in Italy after Sarri's departure for Chelsea, working on the coaching staff at Cagliari and Napoli again alongside future Italy head coach Luciano Spalletti. In 2022 he succeeded Pavel Hapal in Slovakia, becoming the national team's first foreign head coach. He is the country's first national coach from a non-native background.

KEY PLAYER

MILAN ŠKRINIAR

POSITION: Centre-back
CLUB: Paris Saint-Germain FC (FRANCE)
AGE: 29
BORN: 11 February 1995, Žiar Nad Hronom
INTERNATIONAL DEBUT: 27 May 2016 vs Georgia
CAPS: 66 • **GOALS**: 3

Milan Škriniar is one of Slovakia's most experienced and well-tested defenders at international level. He was promoted from the national team age group squads just in time to play at UEFA EURO 2016 in France. He was one of the pillars of the Slovakia team, who finished third in their group at the subsequent pandemic-delayed finals in 2021. Slovakia's captain began his career with MSK Žilina and transferred in 2016 to Italian football with Sampdoria of Genoa and then Internazionale. Škriniar helped Inter win one Serie A league title and both the Coppa Italia and Supercoppa on two occasions. His inspiring leadership saw him appointed as captain of Inter before his departure for French champions Paris Saint-Germain in 2023.

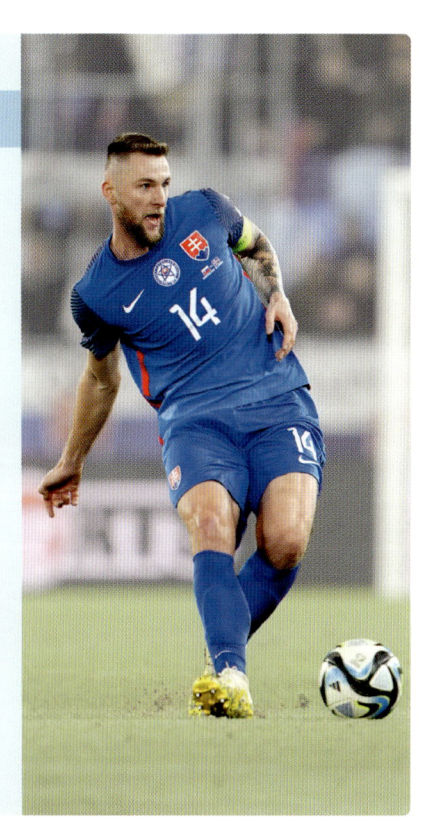

claimed a second goal through Andri Gudjohnsen but the 4-2 win ensured Slovakia's progress to the finals.

Qualification for the finals yet again vindicated the association's appointment of Calzona back in 2022 for what was his first head coach appointment after a decade as a No2 in Italian football. The lessons learned served Slovakia well. Calzona said: "I was never just an assistant wearing the coach's jacket. I was an assistant at the highest level. I gained more experience that way than if I had been to university."

One of Calzona's achievements has been to manage the successful redevelopment of the national squad after the retirement of long-time stalwarts such as defenders Martin Škrtel and Ján Ďurica, plus record marksman Marek Hamšík.

Martin Dúbravka has continued to be the first choice in goal for Slovakia despite vying for the gloves with Nick Pope at Newcastle United in the English Premier League. Defensive pillars in front of him include captain Milan Škriniar and Peter Pekarík, who made his Slovakia national team debut back in December 2006. Pekarík celebrated his 100th cap in 2021. His experience has proved invaluable after his roles at the 2010 World Cup and then at the EUROs in 2016 and 2020.

Another veteran of all three campaigns is midfielder Juraj Kucka. He made his senior debut in 2008 and played in all three of Slovakia's matches at the 2010 World Cup despite not having featured in the qualifying competition. He was also there again at EURO 2016 and 2020.

The main attacking mantle has fallen on 33-year-old Róbert Mak, with more than 75 international appearances to his name. Mak was born in Bratislava and spent four years at the Manchester City academy but without ever achieving a breakthrough into the first team squad. A wandering career path then took him to Germany with Nürnberg, Greece with PAOK, Russia with Zenit Saint Petersburg, Türkiye with Konyaspor, Hungary with Ferencváros and then Sydney FC in Australia.

DID YOU KNOW?

Slovakia failed in their first five attempts to qualify for the finals but have made up for lost time and are now competing for the third time in a row.

GROUP E
ROMANIA

UEFA EURO 2024 in Germany will be Romania's first major finals since UEFA EURO 2016 in France, when they did not progress beyond the group stage. After missing out on qualification for EURO 2020, the team led by coach Edward Iordănescu are on a mission to rebuild their reputation.

The country embraced football before most of its Balkan neighbours, mainly owing to the influence of the country's sovereign, King Carol I, who was a fan. He instigated the formation of a football assocation in 1908 and, having returned to power in 1930 after a forced abdication, he was determined that Romania should enter the first World Cup.

Political reorganisation after the Second World War saw the creation of army team Steaua and police club Dinamo, who dominated the domestic game for decades. In 1986 Steaua became the first club from eastern Europe to win the European Champion Clubs' Cup, defeating Barcelona on penalties in Seville.

At the same time, the national team started to make its presence felt on the international scene. They reached the group stage of the 1970 FIFA World Cup and then the group stage of the 1984 European Championship.

Romania went on to reach three World Cups in a row, between 1990 and 1998, and qualified for the EURO in 1996 and 2000. In Belgium and the Netherlands at EURO 2000, Romania reached the quarter-finals before losing 2-0 to Italy. Group stage finishes followed at the EUROs in 2008 and 2016, when a young

ROMANIA at the UEFA European Championship

1960	Did not qualify
1964	Did not qualify
1968	Did not qualify
1972	Did not qualify
1976	Did not qualify
1980	Did not qualify
1984	Group stage
1988	Did not qualify
1992	Did not qualify
1996	Group stage
2000	Quarter-finals
2004	Did not qualify
2008	Group stage
2012	Did not qualify
2016	Group stage
2020*	Did not qualify

*2020 finals were played in 2021

COACH

EDWARD IORDĂNESCU

Edward Iordănescu has football success in his DNA. He is the son of Anghel Iordănescu, who won the European Champion Clubs' Cup with Steaua Bucharest in 1986 and then, as coach, took Romania to the FIFA World Cup twice and EURO '96. Son Edward followed in his father's footsteps in playing and coaching Steaua. His playing career also took him to Greece and Cyprus with Panionios and Alki Larnaca. He was appointed national team coach in 2022 after two successful coaching spells with CFR Cluj, winning one league title and two domestic cups.

ABOVE: Romania will be making their sixth EURO appearance this summer, with their best finish to date being the quarter-finals at EURO 2000.

KEY PLAYER

NICOLAE STANCIU

POSITION: Midfield
CLUB: Damac FC (SAUDI ARABIA)
AGE: 29
BORN: 7 May 1993, Cricău
INTERNATIONAL DEBUT: 23 March 2016 vs Lithuania
CAPS: 66 · **GOALS:** 14

Nicolae Stanciu, an attacking midfielder or occasional winger, is the most experienced member and captain of the Romania squad who qualified for UEFA EURO 2024 in Germany. Stanciu won six domestic honours while at Unirea Alba Iulia, Vaslui and Steaua Bucharest. In 2016 he became Romania's most expensive footballer when he was sold to Belgium's Anderlecht for €8m. He stayed in Brussels only 18 months before joining Sparta Prague. In 2019 Stanciu played briefly for Saudi Arabia's Al-Ahli before returning to Prague to win the league crown twice in successive seasons with Slavia. After a short spell with the Chinese Super League club Wuhan Three Towns, he moved to his current Saudi club, Damac. Stanciu's national team highlights include appearances at the EURO 2016 finals in France.

Nicolae Stanciu, now Romania's captain, was a bright new member of the national squad.

Midfield is the core of the Romanian national team, with Stanciu both their inspirational captain and most experienced international. Further significant experience is provided by Italy-based Răzvan Marin from Empoli, handy goalscorer Valentin Mihăilă from Parma and Marius Marin from Pisa, plus Alexandru Cicâldău from Türkiye's Konyaspor. Genoa's George Pușcaș provides goals up front, where further talent is at hand in Ianis Hagi, son of Gheorghe Hagi, arguably Romania's greatest ever player.

At the other end of the pitch from the forwards, the goalkeeping role has been contested between veteran Florin Niță from Türkiye's Gaziantep, Horațiu Moldovan from Rapid Bucharest and Ionuț Radu from English Premier League club Bournemouth.

Romania were placed in Pot 3 for the EURO 2024 qualifying draw, which could have meant a tough group. They were ultimately delivered a busy schedule in competition with Switzerland, Israel, Belarus, Kosovo and Andorra. They began positively with wins over Andorra and Belarus before holding Kosovo to a goalless draw in Pristina, then snatching a 2-2 result in Switzerland with two late goals from Italy-based Mihăilă.

Iordănescu's men maintained their proud unbeaten record through the autumn schedule and clinched qualification with a game to spare after beating Israel 2-1 on neutral territory at the Pancho Arena in Felcsút, Hungary. Romania won with goals from Ianis Hagi after ten minutes and George Pușcaș shortly before the final whistle.

Romania then capitalised on home advantage to beat Switzerland 1-0 in Bucharest in the final round of matches and thus top the group. A draw would have been enough to see them through.

DID YOU KNOW?

Romania entered the then European Nations' Cup when it was launched in 1958, but this will be only their sixth appearance at the finals.

Play-offs: Path B
ISRAEL

Israel have yet to make a mark on the UEFA European Championship despite a consistent presence in the qualifiers since becoming a UEFA member in 1991.

This time around, in the qualifying competition for a place in Germany, Israel finished third in Group I, only two points behind Switzerland. A 1-1 draw against Switzerland and then a 2-1 defeat against Romania in the closing stages proved crucial. Both matches had been designated as home ties but Israel were unable to host those ties due to security concerns. The matches had to be switched to the Pancho Aréna in Felcsút, Hungary. Hence Israel's entry into the play-offs relied on their having won Group B2 in the UEFA Nations League. Since May 2022, the team's head coach has been former international Alon Hazan, who scored five goals in 72 appearances between 1990 and 2000, while his club career included a double promotion-winning spell in the English Football League with Watford. Senior players in Hazan's squad in the EURO 2024 qualifying campaign included captain Eli Dasa from Dynamo Moscow in defence and well-travelled Eran Zahavi in attack.

COACH
ALON HAZAN

KEY PLAYER
ERAN ZAHAVI
POSITION: Forward
CLUB: Maccabi Tel-Aviv FC (ISRAEL)
AGE: 36

Israel have a chance to make their mark on the tournament via the play-offs.

Play-offs: Path B
BOSNIA AND HERZEGOVINA

Bosnia and Herzegovina have found the going tougher since rising to 13th in the FIFA men's world ranking in 2013, so their presence in the play-offs is a positive sign.

They have never yet qualified for a UEFA EURO final tournament, although they came close on three occasions, losing in the play-offs in 2012, 2016 and 2020. Bosnia and Herzegovina's one appearance in a major tournament remains the FIFA World Cup in Brazil in 2014, when they were eliminated at the end of the group stage after a victory over Iran and narrow defeats by Argentina and Nigeria. The qualifying tournament for EURO 2024 saw Bosnia and Herzegovina finish fifth in the six-team Group J behind Portugal, Slovakia, Luxembourg and Iceland, albeit well clear of Liechtenstein. They owe their place in the play-offs to their success in the UEFA Nations League, having won Group B3 – ahead of fellow play-offs hopefuls Finland, Montenegro and direct EURO qualifiers Romania. Savo Milošević has been head coach since the closing stages of the qualifying competition last September. He played more than 100 times in attack for the former Yugoslavia, and then Serbia and Montenegro. Milošević was a five-goal golden boot winner at EURO 2000.

COACH
SAVO MILOŠEVIĆ

KEY PLAYER
EDIN DŽEKO
POSITION: Forward
CLUB: Fenerbahçe SK (TÜRKIYE)
AGE: 38

Bosnia and Herzegovina are in the play-offs for the fourth time.

Play-offs: Path B
UKRAINE

Ukraine's footballers reached the play-offs for UEFA EURO 2024 despite the immense challenges posed by the conflict in their country.

The war in Ukraine forced them to play all four of their home matches abroad in Trnava (Slovakia), Wrocław (Poland), Prague (Czechia) and Leverkusen (Germany). They finished third in an already challenging Group C, which featured the EURO 2020 champions and runners-up Italy and England. Everything rested on Ukraine's last match, when they needed to beat Italy. Instead, a 0-0 draw left them in third place. Hence access to the play-offs was provided through their second-place finish behind Scotland in Group B1 of the UEFA Nations League. Ukraine have reached the EURO finals on three previous occasions. They played in the group stage in 2012 and 2016, before progressing even further at EURO 2020, when they lost to England in the quarter-finals. Experience in Serhiy Rebrov's team in EURO 2024 qualifying was provided by defenders Mykola Matviyenko and Vitalii Mykolenko, midfielders Oleksandr Zinchenko, captain Taras Stepanenko, Serhiy Sydorchuk and Ruslan Malinovskyi as well as forward Roman Yaremchuk.

COACH
SERHIY REBROV

KEY PLAYER
OLEKSANDR ZINCHENKO
POSITION: Wingback
CLUB: Arsenal FC (ENGLAND)
AGE: 27

Ukraine missed out on direct qualification at the hands of Italy.

Play-offs: Path B
ICELAND

Iceland surprised European football by reaching the quarter-finals in France in 2016 but then fell short in the play-offs for UEFA EURO 2020.

Iceland's return to the play-offs for EURO 2024 offered them the chance to reach the finals for the second time and make up for not being present at EURO 2020. The main EURO 2024 qualifying competition saw Iceland finish behind Portugal, Slovakia and Luxembourg and ahead of Bosnia and Herzegovina as well as Liechtenstein. Iceland's Norwegian head coach Åge Hareide and his squad owed their presence in the play-offs to their second-place finish in Group B2 of the UEFA Nations League. Hareide's challenge was to mould a team from players who play their club football in Belgium, Denmark, France, Germany, Greece, Italy, Netherlands, Norway, Portugal, Sweden and Wales. Veterans included defenders Victor Pálsson, Sverrir Ingi Ingason and Hörður Björgvin Magnússon, midfielders Jóhann Berg Guðmundsson and captain Aron Gunnarsson, plus forwards Alfreð Finnbogason and Hákon Arnar Haraldsson. The latter pair, plus Gunnarsson, were Iceland's three-goal top scorers in qualifying.

COACH
ÅGE HAREIDE

KEY PLAYER
ALFREÐ FINNBOGASON
POSITION: Forward
CLUB: Eupen FC (BELGIUM)
AGE: 35

Iceland were quarter-finalists in France in 2016.

1996

Magic Moments:
GAZZA GLORY

15 JUNE 1996 / WEMBLEY

England's staging of the 1996 finals saw football "coming home". Even if the hosts did not achieve a first major success since the 1966 FIFA World Cup, they did provide fans with memorable moments. The most thrilling occurred in the group match against the "auld enemy" – Scotland. England held a fragile one-goal lead with the Scots having just missed a penalty when Paul Gascoigne struck decisively with 11 minutes to play. Darren Anderton provided the pass which offered 'Gazza' the inspirational opportunity to clip the ball over defender Colin Hendry with his left foot and volley home with his right. Gascoigne's delighted team-mates marked the moment by enacting an instantly iconic celebration based on a headline-generating incident from a pre-finals party.

RIGHT: Paul Gascoigne volleys the second goal for hosts England in their victory over Scotland in Group A at Wembley during EURO '96.

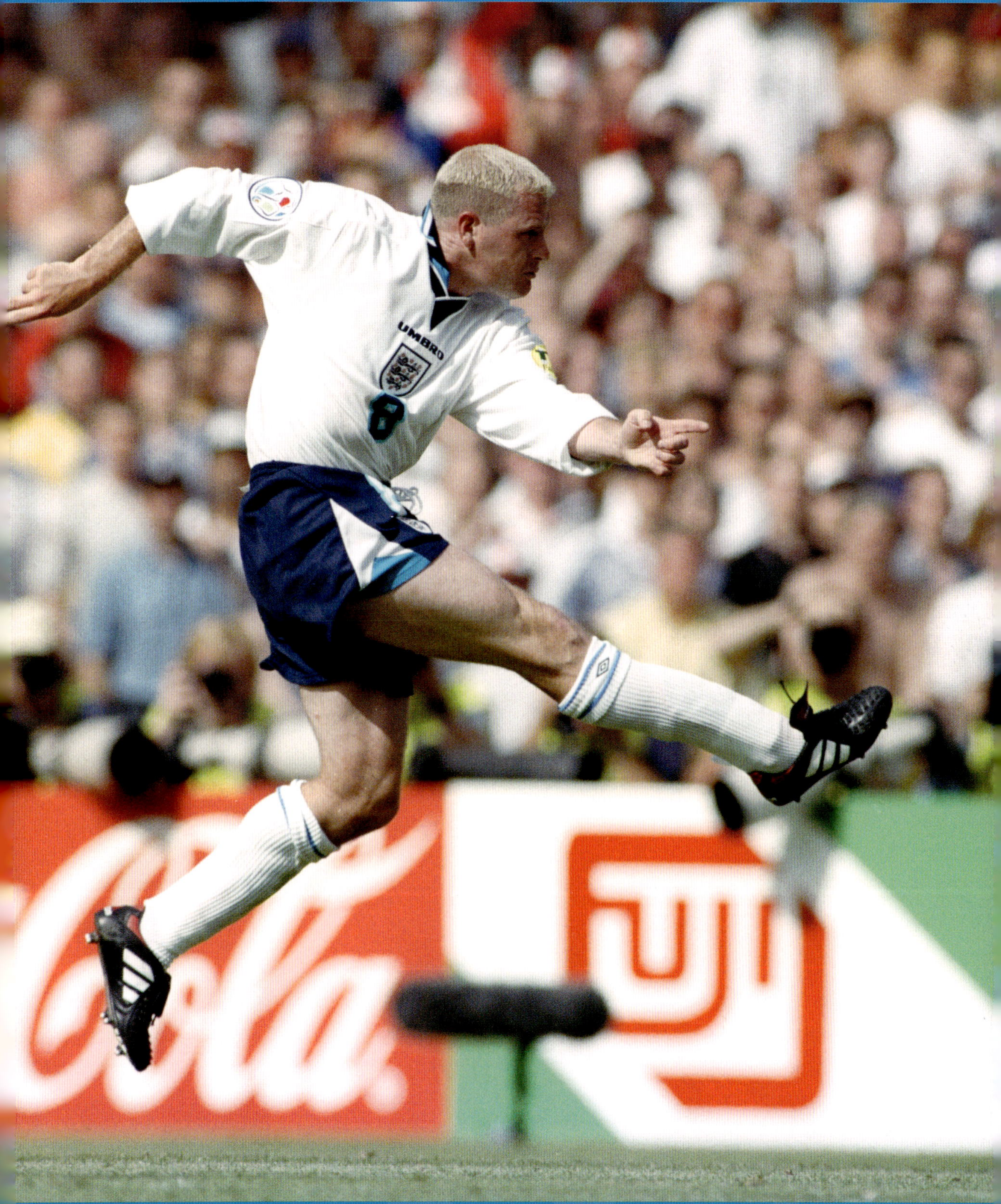
UMBRO

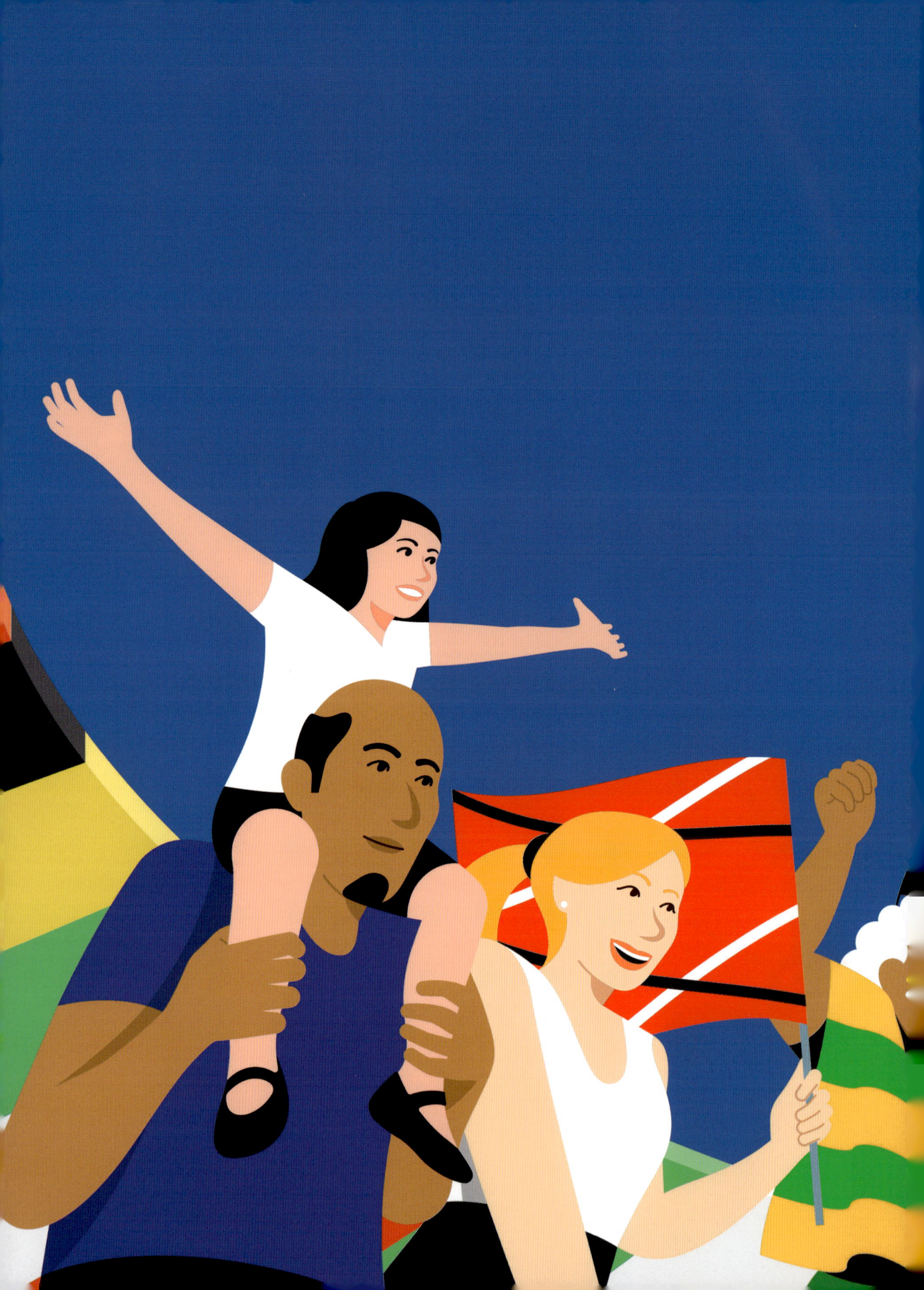

UEFA EURO 2024 GERMANY

GROUP F

Portugal were European champions in 2016, runners-up in 2004 and semi-finalists three times. Czechia (including Czechoslovakia) were champions in 1976, runners-up three times and semi-finalists once. Türkiye were semi-finalists once. At UEFA EURO 2020 Portugal reached the round of 16 and Czechia reached the quarter-finals.

- Türkiye
- Play-off Winner C
- Portugal
- Czechia

GROUP F
TÜRKIYE

Türkiye have been absent from the finals only twice since they made their debut in 1996 and their Italian coach Vincenzo Montella has promised that this time they can "play a great role". That could mean improving on a best-yet semi-final appearance in Austria and Switzerland in 2008.

The passion of Turkish fans is legendary and great clubs such as Beşiktaş JK, Fenerbahçe SK and Galatasaray SK have long been regular and respected campaigners in UEFA's club competitions.

Thus far only Galatasaray have written their name in the honours list, winning the UEFA Cup in 2000. The presence in their team of Brazil goalkeeper Claudio Taffarel and Romania playmaker Gheorghe Hagi underlined the ever-increasing power of Turkish football. Now Türkiye is looking forward to welcoming a major international tournament for the first time, when it shares host rights with Italy for UEFA EURO 2032.

Türkiye's football runs hand in hand with the state's modern history. The game had been introduced by traders and students at the start of the last century before a national federation was created in 1923. Later that same year the modern Turkish republic was proclaimed, with Mustafa Kemal as its first President.

The national team had to wait until after the Second World War to start making their mark on the international stage. Türkiye reached the quarter-finals of the Olympic Games football tournament in 1948 and 1952 then made their FIFA World Cup finals debut in 1954. Türkiye reached the finals in Switzerland thanks to good fortune

ABOVE: Turkey are appearing in the finals for the sixth time after making their debut in 1996 and achieving a best-yet semi-finals finish in 2008.

TÜRKIYE at the UEFA European Championship

1960	Did not qualify
1964	Did not qualify
1968	Did not qualify
1972	Did not qualify
1976	Did not qualify
1980	Did not qualify
1984	Did not qualify
1988	Did not qualify
1992	Did not qualify
1996	Group stage
2000	Quarter-finals
2004	Did not qualify
2008	Semi-finals
2012	Did not qualify
2016	Group stage
2020*	Group stage

*2020 finals were played in 2021

COACH

VINCENZO MONTELLA

Vincenzo Montella first attracted fans' attention with a goal celebration which earned the nickname of Aeroplanino (Little Aeroplane). Montella, 49, scored more than 200 goals for Empoli, Genoa, Sampdoria, Roma and on loan to Fulham in England. He also claimed three goals in 20 games for Italy spread across six years between 1999 and 2005, which included UEFA EURO 2000 when Italy were runners-up on a golden goal to France. He led Milan to the Italian Supercoppa in 2016 and was appointed by Türkiye in 2023 in mid-qualifying campaign after two impressive seasons at Adana Demirspor.

KEY PLAYER

HAKAN ÇALHANOĞLU

POSITION: Midfield
CLUB: FC Internazionale Milano (ITALY)
AGE: 30
BORN: 8 February 1994, Mannheim, Germany
INTERNATIONAL DEBUT: 6 September 2013 vs Andorra
CAPS: 82 • **GOALS**: 17

Hakan Çalhanoğlu will be in familiar surroundings in Germany for EURO 2024, where he was born in Mannheim, the son of a Turkish immigrant family. Coincidentally he first played for his country competitively back in Türkiye when it hosted the 2013 FIFA U-20 World Cup. Months later he made his senior debut in the FIFA World Cup qualifiers. Çalhanoğlu began in Germany with Karlsruhe in the lower divisions then moved into the Bundesliga with Hamburg and Bayer Leverkusen before transferring to Italy with AC Milan in 2017. He spent four seasons as a first-team starter before crossing the city in 2021 to join Internazionale, where he enjoyed trophy-winning success in both the Coppa Italia and Supercoppa, plus a run to the 2023 UEFA Champions League final.

in the drawing of lots after a play-off draw against Spain.

A national championship was launched in 1960, attracting an increasing number of foreign players and coaches. Galatasaray's famous night in Copenhagen saw them become the first Turkish club to win a European competition in the UEFA Cup.

The national team reached EURO for the first time in 1996, made the quarter-finals in 2000 and then the semi-finals at both the World Cup in 2002 and EURO 2008. Since then their ambition has been rewarded by qualifying for the 2016 and 2020 editions, although they did not progress beyond the group stage in either tournament.

Their prospects of qualifying for Germany hung in the balance at one point. Last September, midway through the campaign, the federation decided to replace coach Stefan Kuntz after a 1-1 draw with Armenia and 4-2 friendly match defeat by Japan. Kuntz had been in charge since September 2021 after leading Germany to the UEFA European Under-21 Championship title in 2017 and 2021. His successor was Montella, who knew Turkish football and the players from two impressive seasons coaching Adana Demirspor.

Victories, 1-0 over Croatia and 4-0 over Latvia, guaranteed Türkiye a place in the top two of Group D and thus the certainty of a return to the finals. Yunus Akgün, Kerem Aktürkoğlu and two-goal Cenk Tosun were the all-important men on the scoresheet.

Significant supporting roles in defence have been taken by goalkeepers Uğurcan Çakır and Altay Bayındır plus defenders including Zeki Çelik, Galatasaray's Germany-born Kaan Ayhan and wingback Ferdi Kadıoğlu. A comparatively inexperienced midfield has been relying on veteran Italy-based captain Hakan Çalhanoğlu to create the openings for Cenk and Kerem.

Cenk has experience which should be valuable in the finals. He had been born in Germany and played for them at youth and Under-21 levels before switching in 2013 to Türkiye and leading their attack at EURO 2016.

DID YOU KNOW?

Black Stockings were Türkiye's first football club, founded in 1901. But they were shut down almost at once after police invaded the pitch during their first match.

Play-offs: Path C
GEORGIA

Georgia have never reached a UEFA EURO or FIFA World Cup finals, despite having produced a stream of outstanding individual players.

Georgia completed their EURO 2024 campaign in fourth position behind Spain, Scotland and Norway. The top two went through to Germany for the finals, third-placed Norway missed out entirely, while Georgia reached the play-offs. Their second chance underlined the importance of the UEFA Nations League, in which Georgia had won Group C4, ahead of Bulgaria, North Macedonia and Gibraltar. Their head coach is the former French international defender and Bayern München captain Willy Sagnol. His playing career included a World Cup runners-up medal with France in 2006 in Germany. Sagnol was appointed by the Georgian Football Federation in February 2021. His squad possessed experience in goalkeeper Giorgi Loria, captain Guram Kashia, midfielder Nika Kvekveskiri and one of Europe's most exciting young forwards, Khvicha Kvaratskhelia. Last year the 23-year-old helped Napoli win their first Italian Serie A title in 33 years and he was voted the UEFA Champions League Young Player of the Season for 2022/23.

COACH
WILLY SAGNOL

KEY PLAYER
KHVICHA KVARATSKHELIA
POSITION: Forward
CLUB: Napoli FC (ITALY)
AGE: 23

In reaching the play-offs, Georgia were in pursuit of a major breakthrough.

Play-offs: Path C
GREECE

Greece, European champions in 2004, were aiming to reach the finals for a fifth time after their debut in 1980 and quarter-finals finish last time around in 2012.

The Greeks concluded their UEFA EURO 2024 qualifying campaign third in a tough group that was won by the 2022 FIFA World Cup runners-up France and in which the Netherlands, quarter-finalists in Qatar, were runners-up. Greece progressed into the play-offs courtesy of having topped the table in Group C2 of the UEFA Nations League, where they lost only one of their six matches home and away against Kosovo, Northern Ireland and Cyprus. Entrusted with leading the team was head coach Gus Poyet, a former Uruguay midfielder with wide experience as both a player and a coach in England, France, Greece and Spain as well as further afield in Chile and China. Among Poyet's players, forward Georgios Masouras was outstanding in qualifying, scoring five goals, a total only beaten by France's Kylian Mbappé. The supporting cast included goalkeeper Odysseas Vlachodimos, defenders Giorgos Tzavellas and Kostas Tsimikas, and midfielders Andreas Bouchalakis, captain Tasos Bakasetas and Petros Mantalos.

COACH
GUS POYET

KEY PLAYER
GEORGIOS MASOURAS
POSITION: Forward
CLUB: Olympiacos FC (GREECE)
AGE: 30

Greece hope to reach the finals for the first time in 12 years.

Play-offs: Path C
KAZAKHSTAN

Kazakhstan were admitted to UEFA in 2002. The men's national team have never qualified previously for any major final tournament.

Russian coach Magomed Adiyev was appointed in May 2022 to try to achieve a competitive breakthrough with the Kazakhstan national team. His first challenge was the 2022/23 UEFA Nations League campaign, in which Kazakhstan won Group C3 ahead of Azerbaijan, Slovakia and Belarus. With their confidence boosted as they headed into the UEFA EURO 2024 qualifying competition, they finished in an honourable fourth place in Group H, level on points with third-placed Finland and only four points away from the top spot. The high point of their campaign was their match against Denmark, when Kazakhstan came back from being 2-0 down in the closing stages to win 3-2. They underlined their fighting spirit and counter-attacking threat by claiming another late victory, this time in Northern Ireland. The only goal was scored by Abat Aymbetov, from record champions Astana. Almost all the members of Adiyev's team are drawn from home-based clubs in the Kazakhstan league.

COACH
MAGOMED ADIYEV

KEY PLAYER
ABAT AYMBETOV
POSITION: Forward
CLUB: FC Astana (KAZAKHSTAN)
AGE: 28

Kazakhstan were group winners in the UEFA Nations League.

Play-offs: Path C
LUXEMBOURG

Luxembourg boasts one of the oldest football associations, founded in 1908. But that has meant a long wait in pursuit of a place at a major final tournament.

The Red Lions did not enter the inaugural European Nations' Cup in 1960 but have competed in all 16 campaigns since then. UEFA EURO 2024 qualifying saw their determined efforts rewarded with third place in a six-team Group J. They became one of no fewer than three teams from the group who progressed to the play-offs, together with fourth-placed Iceland and fifth-placed Bosnia and Herzegovina. In the case of Luxembourg, play-off progress was secured through finishing as runners-up to Türkiye in Group C1 of the UEFA Nations League. National technical director is Manuel Cardoni, a former international who scored five goals in 69 international appearances between 1993 and 2004. His squad featured veteran defender and captain Laurent Jans, with 100 caps to his name, as well as forward Gerson Rodrigues, who was the qualifying group's third top scorer with five goals, behind only Portugal's Cristiano Ronaldo and Bruno Fernandes.

COACH
MANUEL CARDONI

KEY PLAYER
GERSON RODRIGUES
POSITION: Forward
CLUB: Sivasspor (TÜRKIYE)
AGE: 28

Luxembourg had history in their sights in the play-offs.

GROUP F
PORTUGAL

Portugal have been serial contenders with Cristiano Ronaldo, one of the greatest footballers of the modern era, inspiring their attack over the past two decades. The UEFA EURO 2016 champions and 2019 Nations League winners raced through to the 2024 finals to underline the force of their ambition.

Ronaldo and Co were so eager to return to the finals fray that they were among the first three nations to qualify simultaneously to join hosts Germany. They did so by winning all their first seven games in Group J.

Slovakia, Luxembourg, Iceland, Bosnia and Herzegovina plus Liechtenstein were left trailing far in Portugal's wake. Perhaps surprisingly the most commanding victory was achieved in Ronaldo's absence, a 9-0 home defeat of Luxembourg. Goalscoring honours were led by Gonçalo Inácio, Gonçalo Ramos and Diogo Jota, who each struck twice.

Ronaldo was back on duty for the 3-2 victory over Slovakia in Porto which confirmed Portugal's ticket for the finals. He scored twice to extend his international record to 127 with the promise of more to come in the finals. As manager Roberto Martínez said: "It's about striving always to be at the highest level."

Portugal's progress was vindication for Martínez only nine months after being appointed. He had been out of work for only weeks after leaving Belgium following the 2022 FIFA World Cup in Qatar. Belgium had been eliminated in the group stage

ABOVE: Portugal have reached the finals eight previous times, always going beyond the group stage and ending up winners in 2016 and runners-up in 2004.

PORTUGAL at the UEFA European Championship

1960	Did not qualify
1964	Did not qualify
1968	Did not qualify
1972	Did not qualify
1976	Did not qualify
1980	Did not qualify
1984	Semi-finals
1988	Did not qualify
1992	Did not qualify
1996	Quarter-finals
2000	Semi-finals
2004	Runners-up
2008	Quarter-finals
2012	Semi-finals
2016	WINNERS
2020*	Round of 16

*2020 finals were played in 2021

COACH

ROBERTO MARTÍNEZ

Roberto Martínez, fresh from managing Belgium at the 2022 FIFA World Cup finals, was appointed the following January by Portugal in succession to Fernando Santos. The 50-year-old Spaniard had begun his career playing for Real Zaragoza, with whom he won the Copa del Rey before moving to British football with Wigan Athletic, Motherwell, Walsall and Swansea City. Martínez began in management with Swansea and guided Wigan to FA Cup success before joining Everton. He led Belgium to the quarter-finals of EURO 2016 and third place at the 2018 FIFA World Cup before falling at the group stage in Qatar.

KEY PLAYER

BRUNO FERNANDES

POSITION: Midfield
CLUB: Manchester United FC (ENGLAND)
AGE: 29
BORN: 8 September 1994, Maia
INTERNATIONAL DEBUT: 10 November 2017 vs Saudi Arabia
CAPS: 63 • **GOALS**: 19

Bruno Fernandes has proved a perpetual danger in midfield in a career which took him from Portugal's Boavista as a teenager to Italy with Novara, Udinese and Sampdoria, back home with Sporting and then to England with Manchester United. He played for Portugal at age group levels and in the team who reached the round of 16 at the 2016 Olympic Games in Rio de Janeiro. Next came the 2018 FIFA World Cup, then the following year Fernandes was named in the Team of the Tournament as Portugal won the 2019 UEFA Nations League. He then provided two goals and three assists during Portugal's run to the quarter-finals of the 2022 World Cup. During the UEFA EURO 2024 qualifiers he contributed one goal and three assists in Portugal's record 9-0 victory over Luxembourg.

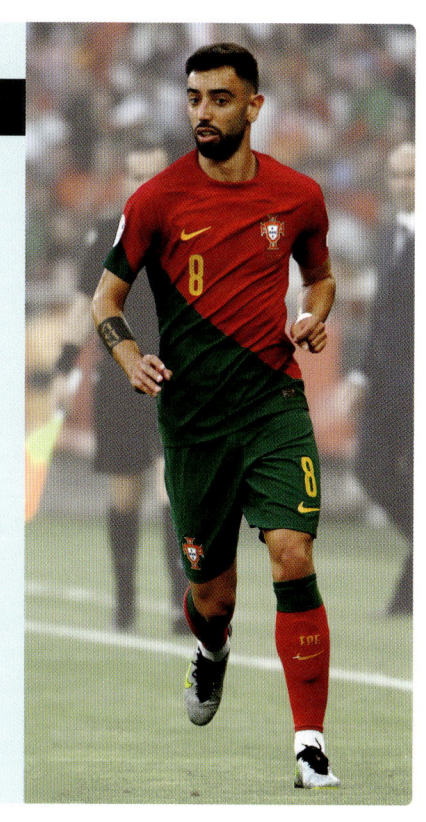

---

while Portugal, under EURO 2016-winning coach Fernando Santos, had reached the quarter-finals before losing to Morocco.

Martínez, on taking up the Portuguese reins, applied a 4-3-3 system with Manchester City's Rúben Dias at the heart of defence. Ahead of him club-mate Bernardo Santos and Manchester United's Bruno Fernandes worked the flanks in midfield alongside yet another English Premier League star in Fulham's João Palhinha.

Up front, Martínez is spoiled for choice for Ronaldo's partners. Apart from Ramos and Jota, Portugal can look to much-travelled João Félix plus Rafael Leão. The latter's brilliance in Italy's Serie A with AC Milan had earned him the iconic No10 once worn by club greats such as Ruud Gullit and Roberto Baggio.

Portugal are no newcomers to the highest sphere of international football. Benfica were the first club to break the grip of Real Madrid on the European Cup in the early 1960s and provided the backbone of the Portugal team who finished third at the World Cup in 1966. Their nine-goal hero was the great Mozambique-born forward Eusébio, the finals' leading marksman.

After a "lost decade" in the 1970s Portugal revived in the 1980s. Porto won the European Cup while a new golden generation won the FIFA World Youth Cups of 1989 and 1991 and star graduate Luís Figo would later be crowned both World and European player of the year.

Porto, under José Mourinho, won the UEFA Cup and UEFA Champions League in 2003 and 2004 to spark a further renewal of confidence. Portugal were runners-up as hosts at EURO 2004 and then fourth at the 2006 World Cup. Now they boasted a new hero in Cristiano Ronaldo, who urged his team-mates on to victory at EURO 2016 from the technical area after having been injured early in the final against hosts France.

DID YOU KNOW?

Fernando Santos managed Portugal for a record 109 matches between 2014 and 2022, including glory at EURO 2016 and the UEFA Nations League in 2019.

GROUP F
CZECHIA

Czechia have maintained a high-profile status in international competition. This will be their seventh successive appearance at this final tournament, the highlight being a runners-up finish in 1996. Previously, Czechoslovakia had been European champions in 1976.

Qualification for the finals in Germany was secured by a second-place slot in Group E behind Albania. The Czechs began confidently with a 3-1 victory over Poland and lost only one of their eight matches, 3-0 away to Albania, with whom they had previously drawn 1-1 at home. That one defeat proved significant at the end of the competition. Czechia and Albania finished level on points but Albania took top spot by virtue of their superior head-to-head record.

Both the outcome and pressure proved a disappointment for coach Jaroslav Šilhavý, who resigned after five years in the role. Šilhavý, 62, had guided Czechia to two EURO tournaments but decided it was time to leave on the high of qualification for Germany.

The team Šilhavý has bequeathed bears on its shoulders the responsibility of living up to a long, proud tradition dating back more than a century to before even Czechoslovakia had been founded. This new nation state identity was created in the wake of the First World War and Czechoslovakia proved to be among Europe's leading football nations throughout the inter-war years.

Sparta and Slavia dominated

CZECHIA at the UEFA European Championship

1960**	Third place
1964**	Did not qualify
1968**	Did not qualify
1972**	Did not qualify
1976**	WINNERS
1980**	Third place
1984**	Did not qualify
1988**	Did not qualify
1992**	Did not qualify
1996	Runners-up
2000	Group stage
2004	Semi-finals
2008	Group stage
2012	Quarter-finals
2016	Group stage
2020*	Quarter-finals

*2020 finals were played in 2021
**1960–92 as Czechoslovakia

COACH

IVAN HAŠEK

Ivan Hašek was appointed at the start of January 2024 for his second stint as national coach, in succession to Jaroslav Šilhavý. Hašek, 60, scored five goals in 60 games as a midfielder between 1984 and 1994 and captained the Czechia team to the quarter-finals of the 1990 World Cup. He played most of his club career with Sparta Prague and was later the national football association president between 2009 and 2011 and, briefly, interim national coach. Hašek then coached club and national teams in Czechia, France, Japan, Gabon, Lebanon, Qatar, Saudi Arabia and United Arab Emirates.

ABOVE: Czechia have a proud record at the UEFA European Championship finals having finished as winners, runners-up and semi-finalists across the years since 1960.

KEY PLAYER

TOMÁŠ SOUČEK

POSITION: Midfield
CLUB: West Ham United FC (ENGLAND)
AGE: 29
BORN: 27 February 1995, Havlíčkův Brod
INTERNATIONAL DEBUT: 15 November 2016 vs Denmark
CAPS: 66 • **GOALS**: 12

Tomáš Souček has been a midfield mainstay of the national team for seven years. He has been awarded player of the year by the Czech sports media three times and was awarded the Jan Masaryk Silver Medal for his role as a national sporting ambassador in 2021. Souček began his career with Slavia Prague, who sold him in 2020 to West Ham United for £20m. Souček can play both as a defensive or attacking midfielder and was a key figure in West Ham's UEFA Europa Conference League success in 2023. The Hammers beat Fiorentina to land their first trophy in 43 years. Souček played for Czechia at youth level before making his senior debut against Denmark in 2016. He was a member of the Czech squad who reached the quarter-finals of UEFA EURO 2020 and was subsequently appointed captain.

the Mitropa Cup – a precursor for continental club competitions featuring central European sides – and the national team were runners-up in the 1930 Central European International Cup and again at the 1934 FIFA World Cup. Superstars of the eras included goalkeeper František Plánička and forwards Oldřich Nejedlý, Antonín Puč and Josef 'Pepi' Bican.

After the Second World War the army club Dukla, led by the great midfielder Josef Masopust, provided the foundation for a national team who were runners-up to Brazil at the World Cup in 1962. Czechoslovakia were also among the early powers at the EURO. They finished third at the inaugural finals in France, won a dramatic final against West Germany in 1976 after a penalty shoot-out and finished third again in 1980 – once more proving adept at penalties in a shoot-out victory over hosts Italy in Naples.

A quarter-final appearance at the 1990 World Cup in Italy proved an international swansong before the country was separated into the Czech Republic and Slovakia. Runners-up spot at EURO '96 in England and a semi-final appearance in 2004 proved that Czechia remained a power in the game.

Carrying on this tradition is a squad drawn from clubs in England, Germany, Greece, Italy, Netherlands, Poland, Portugal, Slovakia and the United States. Experienced defender Vladimír Coufal plays his club football alongside national team captain Tomáš Souček at West Ham United in the English Premier League and experienced partners at the back in qualifying included Jakub Brabec and Tomáš Holeš.

Souček is the versatile central force in midfield, alongside Lukáš Masopust, Lukáš Provod and Michal Sadílek. Indeed, captain Souček was Czechia's three-goal top scorer in the qualifying campaign followed by two-goal Ladislav Krejčí.

DID YOU KNOW?

Czechia, including their Czechoslovakian forerunners, have reached the finals ten times including all of the past seven tournaments.

2012

Magic Moments:
SHEVCHENKO IN STYLE

11 JUNE 2012 / KYIV

The EURO was staged in eastern Europe for the first time in 2012 with Ukraine and Poland sharing the honour. This was the third co-hosting of the finals after 2000 and 2008. Poland opened up with a 1-1 draw against Greece before Ukraine made history of their own in Kyiv and thrilled 64,000 home fans with a 2-1 victory over Sweden. Appropriately, captain Andriy Shevchenko, Ukraine's greatest player, headed both goals as Ukraine recovered from falling a goal behind early in the second half. Shevchenko, 35, had overcome serious injuries to regain fitness in time for the tournament. He retired from national team football after the finals, having scored a then record 48 goals in 111 appearances for his country since his debut in 1995.

RIGHT: Ukraine captain Andriy Shevchenko thrills his home fans in Kyiv by heading the winning goal of the co-hosts' opening match against Sweden in 2012.

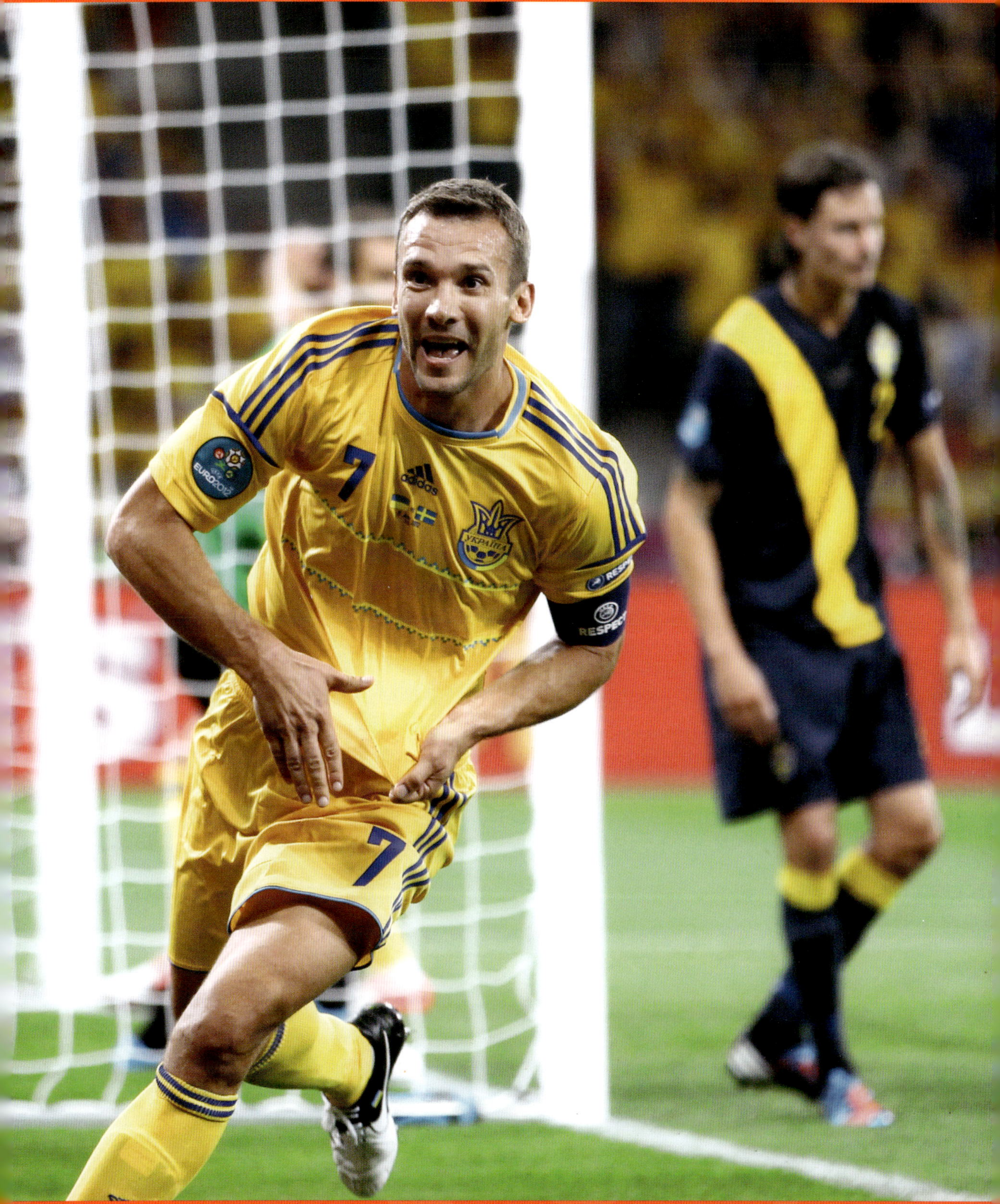
adidas
RESPECT

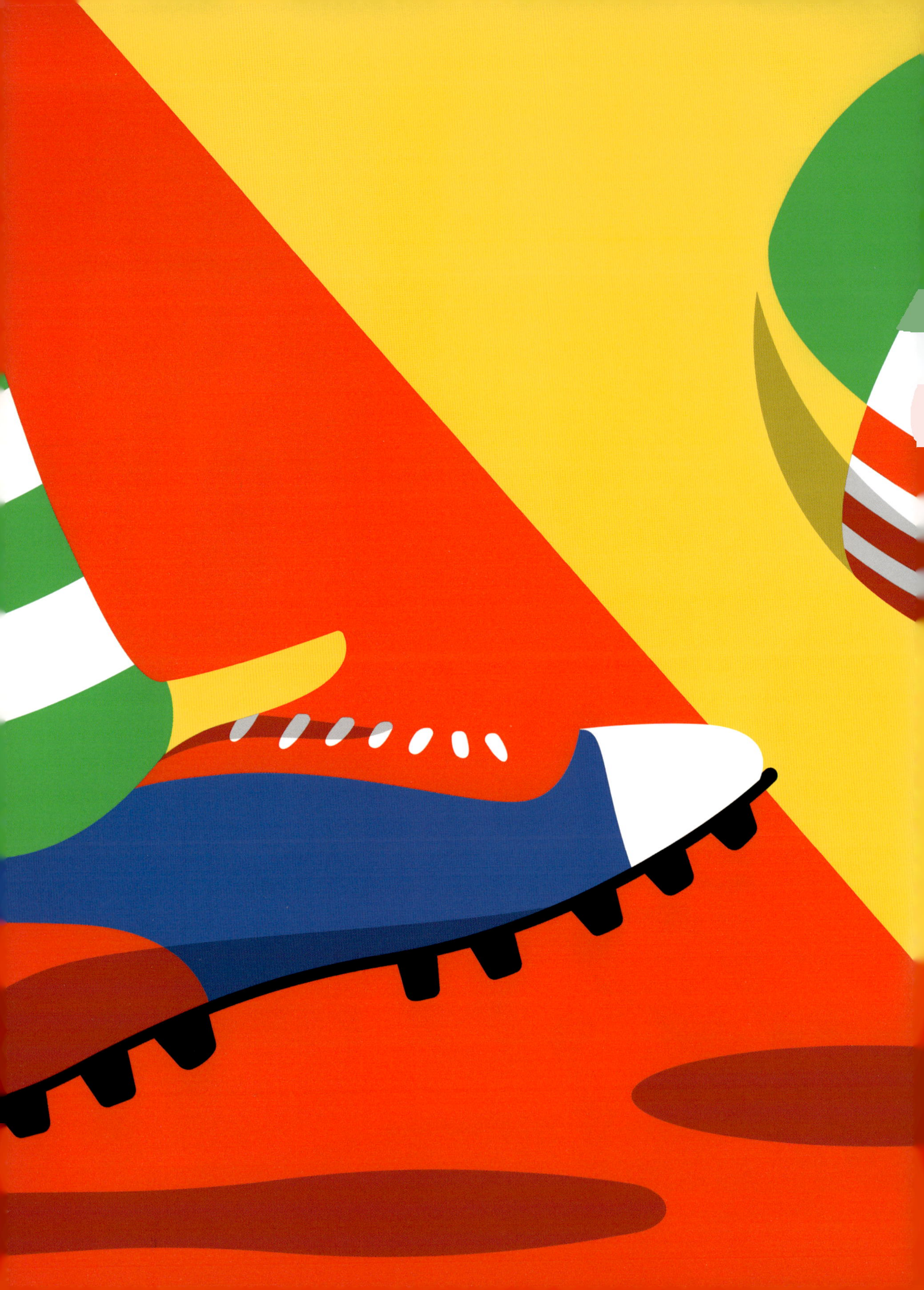

EURO 2024 SUPERSTARS

Europe is home to as great a wealth of footballing talent as any other region of the international game, courtesy of the tradition of its nations and the strength of the club game. Europe's superstar players, from goalkeepers such as Gianluigi Donnarumma to goalscorers such as Harry Kane, are admired and followed by fans throughout the world for their talent, their past acomplishments and their achievements to come.

KEVIN DE BRUYNE

Kevin De Bruyne's skill, vision, work ethic and goals from midfield have been key factors in the Belgian national team's high-profile status in European and world football, as well as in his club Manchester City's success in both UEFA Champions League and English Premier League.

POSITION: Midfielder
CLUB: Manchester City FC (ENGLAND)
BORN: 28 June 1991
INTERNATIONAL DEBUT: 11 August 2010 vs Finland
CAPS: 99
GOALS: 26

The career of a future world football superstar began with his home-town KVE Drongen in central Belgium. Quickly De Bruyne progressed up the ladder with KAA Gent and KRC Genk, with whom he became national champion. Then it was on to Chelsea in the English Premier League before a move to Germany on loan with Werder Bremen and a €30m transfer to VfL Wolfsburg.

De Bruyne's outstanding displays for both club and country earned a return to English football with Manchester City in 2015. The €65m fee was then a record for a Belgian footballer. The subsequent nine years under first Manuel Pellegrini but then, significantly, Pep Guardiola, have seen De Bruyne's career striding from strength to strength.

He and City together have won more than a dozen domestic trophies as well as the UEFA Champions League. Individual honours have included awards as footballer of the year in Germany, sportsman of the year in Belgium, Premier League player of the season and UEFA Champions League midfielder of the season.

De Bruyne played for Belgium at Under-18, Under-19 and Under-21 levels before making his senior debut in August 2010 away to Finland. His first goal for his country followed two months later away to Serbia. Subsequently De Bruyne established himself in the starting line-up ahead of the 2014 FIFA World Cup.

The quarter-finals proved the stopping point for Belgium in Brazil as well as at both EURO 2016 and 2020. In between, De Bruyne and his team-mates went one step further, eventually finishing third at the 2018 World Cup in Russia.

RIGHT: Kevin De Bruyne played 19 times for Belgium's age group teams before stepping up in 2010.

GIANLUIGI DONNARUMMA

Gianluigi Donnarumma became one of the giants of European football when still only 22 by saving two penalties to edge Italy to their shoot-out victory over England in the final of UEFA EURO 2020. Remarkably, he had made his senior debut for the Azzurri almost five years earlier.

POSITION: Goalkeeper
CLUB: Paris Saint-Germain FC (FRANCE)
BORN: 25 February 1999
INTERNATIONAL DEBUT: 1 September 2016 vs France
CAPS: 60
GOALS: 0

As a teenager Donnarumma, from Castellammare di Stabia on the Bay of Naples, had followed brother Antonio to AC Milan in 2013. His potential saw him playing with and against teams in higher age groups. Donnarumma turned professional at 16 and later made his Serie A debut against Sassuolo in 2015. The following January he became the youngest player to start a derby against Internazionale.

A talent for saving penalties was soon evident. Donnarumma stopped his first at senior level against Torino at the start of the 2016/17 season and another in a shoot-out victory over Juventus in the Italian Super Cup in Doha. A year later his safe hands and deft feet saw him become the youngest Milan player to reach 100 senior appearances and then the youngest to reach the same total in Serie A.

Donnarumma's personality and reflexes accelerated his progress through all the stages of the Italian national youth teams. He then made his senior debut as a substitute for veteran hero Gianluigi Buffon in a friendly match against France. At 17 years, 189 days, Donnarumma thus became Italy's youngest-ever goalkeeper.

Donnarumma starred in all Italy's matches during EURO 2020. Crucially he saved shoot-out penalties in the victories over Spain in the semi-final and England in the final. He also collected the best player award. That summer he transferred from Milan to Paris Saint-Germain, with whom he won French league titles. Donnarumma also helped Italy to third-place finishes at both the 2021 and 2023 UEFA Nations League finals.

RIGHT: Gianluigi Donnarumma was hailed as the most outstanding player at the EURO 2020 finals.

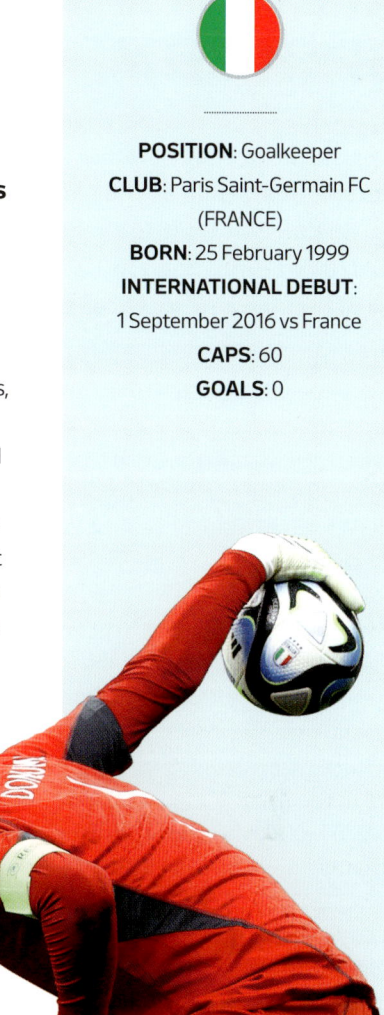

CHRISTIAN ERIKSEN

Christian Eriksen first made a name for himself on the international stage as the youngest player at the FIFA World Cup finals in South Africa in 2010 when still only 18 years, four months old. Since then he has established himself as not only one of Denmark's most creative but most-capped players.

POSITION: Midfielder
CLUB: Manchester United FC (ENGLAND)
BORN: 14 February 1992
INTERNATIONAL DEBUT: 3 March 2010 vs Austria
CAPS: 128
GOALS: 40

The playmaker's club career has taken him from Odense Boldklub to the Netherlands with Ajax, to England with Tottenham, Italy with Internazionale and back to England with Brentford and Manchester United. A classic No10, he has been three times a Dutch champion, once a Serie A winner, a cup winner with United and a UEFA Champions League runner-up with Tottenham in 2019.

Whatever his club, Eriksen has remained a fixture in the Denmark midfield when fit. He proved himself as both creator and marksman on the road to the 2018 World Cup. Eriksen scored eight times in the qualifying group games then a hat-trick in a play-off against the Republic of Ireland. Victory sent Eriksen and his team-mates to Russia, where their campaign ended in a penalty shoot-out defeat by Croatia in the round of 16.

In October 2020 Eriksen celebrated becoming the youngest Dane to reach 100 caps by scoring the decisive goal in a 1-0 win over England at Wembley. Eight months later, however, his career was interrupted after he suffered a cardiac arrest during a UEFA EURO 2020 group stage game against Finland in Copenhagen.

Eriksen underwent surgery to fit a defibrillator and resumed his club career in impressive fashion in the English Premier League with Brentford and then Manchester United. In the meantime, in March 2022, he marked his comeback for Denmark with a goal against the Netherlands.

RIGHT: Christian Eriksen was the youngest Dane to reach a century of international appearances.

İLKAY GÜNDOĞAN

İlkay Gündoğan has proved himself one of the most versatile midfielders in European football. He earned his status as Germany's footballer of the year in 2023 with his work rate between the penalty boxes and timing of his runs to create goalscoring opportunities for club and country.

Gündoğan's family come from Dursunbey in the Marmara region of Turkey, though he was born and brought up in Gelsenkirchen in the heart of the German Ruhr. Between 2008 and 2012 he played 17 times for Germany at different youth levels. After transferring from Nürnberg to Borussia Dortmund, Gündoğan made his senior international debut, in October 2011.

In March 2013 his old fans in Nuremberg witnessed Gündoğan's first international goal in a 4-1 victory over Kazakhstan in a FIFA World Cup qualifier. Unfortunately his progress was interrupted by serious injuries at the start of the 2013/14 season and again in May 2016. The second injury forced him to miss UEFA EURO 2016 in France.

Gündoğan is still waiting to make a significant tournament mark with Germany. He was a member of the squad eliminated in the group stage of the World Cup in Russia in 2018 and then in the round of 16 at the subsequent EURO.

The 2022 World Cup in Qatar brought further disappointment, but this was a massive contrast compared with Gündoğan's outstanding achievements at club level. He was a German champion in 2012 with Borussia Dortmund before becoming the first signing made by Manchester City's newly appointed manager, Pep Guardiola, in 2016. That judgement was vindicated by Gündoğan's role in winning five English Premier League titles plus the UEFA Champions League before his move to Barcelona in 2023. Having EURO 2024 on home soil comes at a great time for this star.

RIGHT: İlkay Gündoğan won UEFA's top club prize in 2023 and is now pursuing the national team equivalent.

POSITION: Midfielder
CLUB: FC Barcelona (SPAIN)
BORN: 24 October 1990
INTERNATIONAL DEBUT: 11 October 2011 vs Belgium
CAPS: 73
GOALS: 18

HARRY KANE

England captain Harry Kane is his country's all-time leading scorer. The 30-year-old Bayern München star has proved himself, over his nine-year international career, as the ideal forward. He mixes the position's traditional leadership role with the finesse and vision essential in the modern game.

POSITION: Forward
CLUB: FC Bayern München (GERMANY)
BORN: 28 July 1993
INTERNATIONAL DEBUT: 27 March 2015 vs Lithuania
CAPS: 89
GOALS: 62

Kane claimed the England record by scoring his 54th goal for his country in a EURO qualifying victory over Italy in March last year. The goal marked Kane's 81st international appearance and surpassed the 53-goal tally set by former team-mate Wayne Rooney in 2015.

Kane steadily worked his way up the England ladder, representing his country at Under-17, Under-19, Under-20 and Under-21 levels. He scored at the FIFA U-20 World Cup and was a regular with the Under-21s before making his senior debut against Lithuania as a second-half substitute in a UEFA EURO 2016 qualifying match. Kane needed only 90 seconds to open his goalscoring account. His first start for the senior team followed days later in a 1-1 draw with Italy in Turin.

He was appointed England captain in May 2018 and led by example at that year's FIFA World Cup, taking England to the semi-finals and finishing as the tournament's top scorer with six goals.

In 2010 Kane turned professional with Tottenham Hotspur and had loan spells with four other clubs before returning to make his Premier League debut in April 2014. He scored a club record 280 goals for Spurs in all competitions. Kane contributed four goals in Tottenham's run to the UEFA Champions League final in 2019 and was the Premier League top scorer three times before transferring to Bayern in the summer of last year. He cost the Bavarians a German record fee of €110m.

Kane left the Premier League with 213 goals, behind Alan Shearer (260) and ahead of Rooney (208).

RIGHT: Harry Kane has proved himself a prolific goalscorer at club and national team levels.

KYLIAN MBAPPÉ

Kylian Mbappé's explosive brilliance has lit up international football ever since his France debut seven years ago. In 2018, aged 19, he was the youngest player to score in a FIFA World Cup final since Pelé in 1958, and in 2022 he was the leading marksman at the finals in Qatar with eight goals.

Mbappé was born and brought up in Bondy, a north-eastern suburb of Paris, and took his first steps at local AS Bondy where his father, Wilfried, was a coach. His talent brought a move to Monaco, for whom he was the youngest debutant aged 16 years, 347 days.

Goals, including hat-tricks, followed as Mbappé led Monaco to the French league title and UEFA Champions League semi-finals in 2017. He then joined Paris Saint-Germain for €180m, becoming the second-most expensive footballer of all time.

Mbappé lived up to expectations by firing PSG to five Ligue 1 titles as well as two trebles of league, French Cup and League Cup plus a runners-up spot in the 2020 Champions League. His mixture of skill, pace and goals earned national player of the year awards in 2018, 2019 and 2022.

With France, Mbappé won the 2016 UEFA European Under-19 Championship and made his senior debut a year later, still only 18. Mbappé became the youngest French player to score at a World Cup during Les Bleus' triumphant 2018 campaign and the second teenager, after Pelé, to score in the final. His four goals and overall performances were rewarded with the Best Young Player award.

Mbappé has continued to prove unstoppable. In 2021 he struck France's winning goal against Spain in the final of the UEFA Nations League. Then, a year later, he became the second player, after England's Geoff Hurst in 1966, to score a hat-trick – despite defeat – in the FIFA World Cup final.

RIGHT: Kylian Mbappé was voted France's top player three times in five years between 2018 and 2022.

POSITION: Forward
CLUB: Paris Saint-Germain FC (FRANCE)
BORN: 20 December 1998
INTERNATIONAL DEBUT: 25 March 2017 vs Luxembourg
CAPS: 75
GOALS: 46

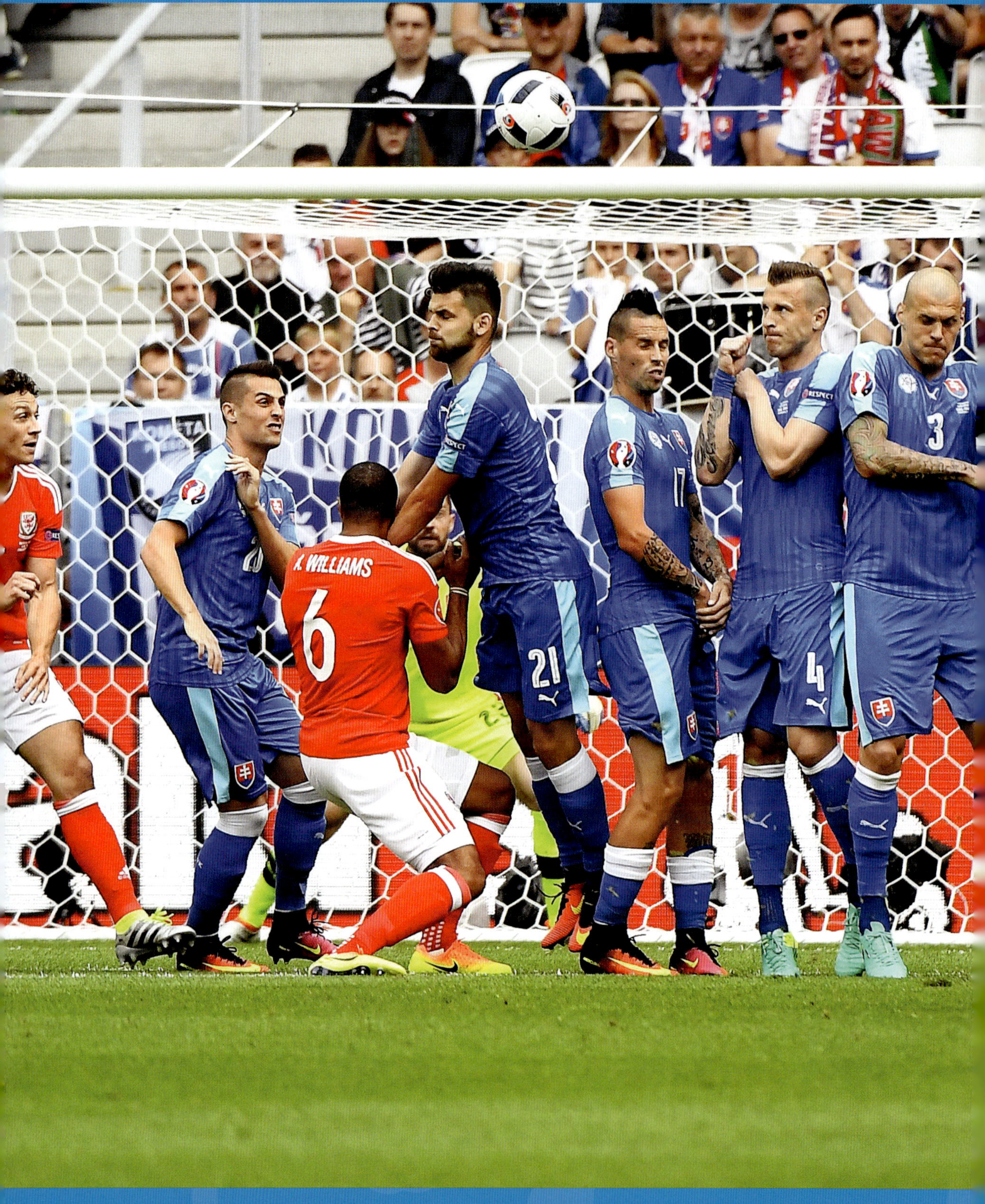
A. WILLIAMS

2016

Magic Moments:
WALES' WONDERS

11 JUNE 2016 / BORDEAUX

Wales, inspired by captain Gareth Bale, marked their first appearance in a major tournament for 58 years by reaching the semi-finals in France. Previously they had not been seen at this level since the quarter-finals of the FIFA World Cup in 1958 in Sweden. The Red Dragons went one round better in France after the perfect start with a 2-1 victory over Slovakia. Bale, who had just won the second of an eventual five UEFA Champions Leagues with Real Madrid, set Wales on their way by opening the scoring after only ten minutes. He would score again in Wales' games against England and Russia on the road to the knockout stage. Northern Ireland and Belgium were overcome before the Welsh adventure came to an end against Portugal in the semi-finals.

LEFT: Gareth Bale, from a free-kick, provides EURO finals newcomers Wales with a perfect start in their 2-1 group stage victory over Slovakia in 2016.

ALEKSANDAR MITROVIĆ

Aleksandar Mitrović is Serbia's all-time top scorer after a decade in which he has brought not only goals but leadership. Mitrović excelled as a teenager at youth levels and has been voted twice as Serbia's footballer of the year.

POSITION: Forward
CLUB: Al Hilal FSC (SAUDI ARABIA)
BORN: 16 September 1994
INTERNATIONAL DEBUT: 7 June 2013 vs Belgium
CAPS: 87
GOALS: 57

Mitrović collected his first international prize in 2013 when Serbia won the UEFA European Under-19 Championship and he was voted best player. His powerful and direct style saw him step up swiftly into the Under-21s before a senior debut in June 2013 against Belgium in Brussels in a 2014 FIFA World Cup qualifying tie. Mitrović's first senior goal arrived three months later against Croatia and his first hat-trick in a World Cup warm-up friendly against Bolivia in June 2018.

Serbia and Mitrović failed to progress beyond the group stage in Russia and missed out on UEFA EURO 2020. Mitrović responded to the disappointment by sending Serbia to the 2022 World Cup finals in Qatar. He scored eight goals in qualifying with the most important being a last-minute winner against Portugal in the concluding group match. Mitrović struck twice in the finals before Serbia's campaign ended at the first hurdle.

Mitrović hails from the town of Smederevo, some 30 miles from Belgrade, where he turned professional with Partizan in 2012. He was a league champion in his first full season to earn a transfer to Belgium with Anderlecht, for whom the goals continued to flow. Mitrović added a Belgian league title before transferring to the English Premier League in 2015.

Three years followed at Newcastle United before Mitrović moved to Fulham, then in the Championship, and claimed a modern second-tier record haul of 43 goals to lead the London club back into the top flight. He joined Al Hilal last year for £50m.

RIGHT: Aleksandar Mitrović made his reputation by leading Serbia to the European U19 crown in 2013.

LUKA MODRIĆ

Luka Modrić, Croatia's long-serving captain and playmaker, has been one of the most consistently bright stars in world football for more than a decade. He was hailed as the UEFA men's player of the year in 2018 after captaining Croatia to runners-up spot at the FIFA World Cup finals in Russia.

POSITION: Midfielder
CLUB: Real Madrid (SPAIN)
BORN: 9 September 1985
INTERNATIONAL DEBUT: 1 March 2006 vs Argentina
CAPS: 172
GOALS: 24

Modrić's ability to link defence and attack has secured a host of trophies, while his remarkable fitness levels and longevity have earned the admiration of team-mates and opponents alike.

Dinamo Zagreb was the launchpad for a magnificent club career. Modrić was three times a Croatia league champion and twice a domestic cup winner before transferring to Tottenham Hotspur of the English Premier League in 2008, and then Real Madrid in 2012 for what turned out to be a bargain €30m.

Modrić, with Madrid, has celebrated silverware on 23 occasions, including five victories in both the UEFA Champions League and FIFA Club World Cup plus four UEFA Super Cups. On 11 occasions he has been hailed as Croatia's footballer of the year.

In 2018, when he was best player at the FIFA World Cup, Modrić also won the Best FIFA Men's Player and Ballon d'Or awards. This saw him become the first man in more than a decade to break the awards duopoly of Lionel Messi and Cristiano Ronaldo.

Modrić had been 20 on his senior Croatia debut against Argentina in March 2006. Three months later he made a World Cup finals debut in Germany and was then at the heart of the action as Croatia reached the EURO 2008 quarter-finals.

Ten years later Modrić was appointed captain for Croatia's memorable 2018 World Cup campaign. He and his team-mates followed up by finishing third at the 2022 FIFA World Cup and runners-up at the 2023 UEFA Nations League.

RIGHT: Luka Modrić has won all the major individual prizes for his inspirational leadership of Croatia.

JAN OBLAK

Jan Oblak is one of the most outstanding and highly ranked goalkeepers in world football. He is captain of Slovenia's national team and has been hailed as his country's footballer of the year on six occasions, after demonstrating both his shot-stopping reflexes and command of his penalty area.

Oblak played senior club football in Slovenia only briefly as a teenager with Olimpija Ljubljana. His potential earned attention from clubs in Italy and England and then a transfer to Portugal's most successful team, Benfica. Oblak, still then only 17, was sent out to gain experience on loan to Beira-Mar, Olhanense, União de Leiria and Rio Ave.

In 2013 Oblak was recalled to the Estádio do Sport Lisboa e Benfica and, only one year later, helped inspire the Eagles of Lisbon to a record tenth domestic double. That season also saw Oblak and Benfica win the Portuguese League Cup and finish runners-up on penalties to Sevilla in the UEFA Europa League final in Turin. His brilliance in both domestic and international competition earned Oblak an immediate further transfer to Atlético. The £20m fee made Oblak, at the time, the most expensive goalkeeper ever in La Liga.

Oblak's talent was an important factor in Atlético's own subsequent successes. They won the UEFA Europa League and UEFA Super Cup in 2018 and the Spanish league in 2021. Oblak's secure handling and consistently fine form has seen him honoured with the Zamora trophy as best goalkeeper in La Liga on five occasions. He was also voted the Spanish league's player of the season in 2021.

Oblak played 25 times for Slovenia at youth and Under-21 levels before making his senior debut against Norway in a FIFA World Cup qualifying tie in September 2012. Three years later he became first choice and was appointed captain in 2019.

RIGHT: Jan Oblak is one of the most outstanding keepers in Spain and captains his national team.

POSITION: Goalkeeper
CLUB: Club Atlético de Madrid (SPAIN)
BORN: 7 January 1993
INTERNATIONAL DEBUT:
11 September 2012 vs Norway
CAPS: 62
GOALS: 0

RODRI

Rodri has established himself with Spain and Manchester City as a high-class example of how to fill the role of midfield anchor, which has become pivotal in international football. The rewards for his vision and game intelligence have been evidenced by a dozen titles on behalf of his clubs and country.

POSITION: Midfielder
CLUB: Manchester City FC (ENGLAND)
BORN: 22 June 1996
INTERNATIONAL DEBUT: 21 March 2018 vs Germany
CAPS: 48
GOALS: 1

Rodrigo Hernández Cascante achieved more last season, 2022/23, than many outstanding players manage in their full careers. At the heart of Manchester City's national and international campaigns he was rewarded with four major trophies – the UEFA Champions League and UEFA Super Cup plus the English Premier League and the FA Cup.

Rodri then helped Spain qualify for UEFA EURO 2024, with City manager Pep Guardiola heading a queue of admirers by describing him as "the best midfielder in Europe."

Rodri, born and brought up in Madrid, started out at Atlético but made his name instead with Villarreal. Atlético had to pay €20m to bring him back in 2018 and he made an immediate mark, as his debut brought victory over neighbours Real Madrid in the UEFA Super Cup.

Less than a year later he became City's then most expensive signing at £62m and achieved yet another debut success in the 2019 FA Community Shield.

One success followed another at club level while, simultaneously, Rodri enhanced his national team reputation. He had played for Spain at Under-16, Under-19 and Under-21 levels before celebrating his senior debut as a substitute in a 1-1 draw with Germany in 2018.

However, success to match his club achievements has eluded him – so far. Rodri was a member of the Spanish squad defeated on penalties both by Italy in the semi-finals of UEFA EURO 2020 and by Morocco in the round of 16 at the FIFA World Cup in 2022.

RIGHT: Rodri was a four-time trophy winner with Manchester City in the 2022/23 season.

CRISTIANO RONALDO

Cristiano Ronaldo has amassed the most phenomenal record of any European footballer in this or any other era of the game. He is the world's most-capped male footballer and all-time leading international marksman, while his trophy and awards hauls at both club and individual levels are the stuff of legend.

POSITION: Forward
CLUB: Al-Nassr FC (SAUDI ARABIA)
BORN: 5 February 1985
INTERNATIONAL DEBUT: 20 August 2003 vs Kazakhstan
CAPS: 205
GOALS: 128

The achievements of Cristiano Ronaldo dos Santos Aveiro have earned him FIFA's top men's player prize on seven occasions and Portugal's player of the year award four times. The airport in his native Madeira has been renamed in his honour.

'CR7' has claimed more than 50 individual awards among a shower of trophies garnered at the the UEFA Champions League (five times), FIFA Club World Cup (four times) with Manchester United and Real Madrid, as well as leading his country to success at UEFA EURO 2016 and the inaugural UEFA Nations League in 2019.

Along the way Ronaldo also became the only player to be crowned as the leading league marksman in England (with United), in Spain (with Madrid) and in Italy (with Juventus).

Portugal's captain was 18 in August 2003 when he made his senior debut against Kazakhstan. In 2021, some 18 years later, Ronaldo's drive for success saw him break the men's international scoring record with his 110th and 111th goals in a 2-1 win against the Republic of Ireland. He followed up in March last year by surpassing the national team appearances record of Kuwait's Bader Al-Mutawa on his 197th outing for Portugal.

In between he became, in Qatar, the first male player to score in five FIFA World Cups just as he had become the first man to score in five editions of the UEFA EURO. Following the 2022 World Cup, Ronaldo embarked on a new adventure with Al-Nassr in Saudi Arabia after his second spell with Manchester United.

RIGHT: Cristiano Ronaldo has broken all possible individual records with Portugal.

DOMINIK SZOBOSZLAI

Dominik Szoboszlai is the latest figurehead for a great Hungarian football tradition stretching back a century. This has included the FIFA World Cup runners-up of 1938, the Magical Magyars of the early 1950s, Olympic champion teams and a host of inspirational players and innovative coaches.

POSITION: Midfielder
CLUB: Liverpool FC (ENGLAND)
BORN: 25 October 2000
INTERNATIONAL DEBUT: 21 March 2019 vs Slovakia
CAPS: 38
GOALS: 10

Szoboszlai, despite his young age, has already established himself as captain of Hungary and he has been the country's most expensive player twice over. Firstly, he cost RB Leipzig of the German Bundesliga €20m when he joined from Salzburg, then his valuation escalated to €70m on his transfer to Liverpool and the English Premier League last year.

Those transfers vindicated the many admiring assessments made of Szoboszlai while he was still a teenager. He captained Hungary's Under-17s at the age of 15 and, in January 2020, made the UEFA.com list of young stars in the making.

Szoboszlai, from the historic city of Székesfehérvár, launched his teenage career with Hungarian clubs Fehérvár, Főnix Gold, MTK and then Austria's Liefering, a nursery club for Salzburg.

Aged 17 he made his Austrian Bundesliga debut and, in 2020, a meteoric rise saw him hailed as best player in the league. Szobolszai moved to Leipzig in 2021 and celebrated their first major trophy success in the German Cup in 2022. Liverpool bought him a year later.

Szoboszlai was still with Salzburg when he made his debut and scored his first goal for Hungary's senior national team. Later, he struck the extra-time winner in a play-off against Iceland which propelled Hungary to UEFA EURO 2020. Unfortunately injury prevented him playing in the finals. Hungary failed to reach the FIFA World Cup in Qatar, so EURO 2024 should see their young captain make a long-overdue debut on a major international stage.

RIGHT: Dominik Szoboszlai can make up for lost time after missing UEFA EURO 2020 through injury.

VIRGIL VAN DIJK

At UEFA EURO 2024 Virgil van Dijk will be aiming to make up for lost time in terms of European tournament football. He made his senior national team debut in 2015, but the Netherlands failed to qualify for EURO 2016 and then a knee injury forced him to miss the delayed 2020 finals.

POSITION: Centre-back
CLUB: Liverpool FC (ENGLAND)
BORN: 8 July 1991
INTERNATIONAL DEBUT: 10 October 2015 vs Kazakhstan
CAPS: 64
GOALS: 7

Van Dijk, an inspirational team leader as well as central defensive commander, has won a series of trophies in Scotland and England since launching his career at home with Groningen. He won the Scottish league twice and league cup with Celtic before flying south to the English Premier League with Southampton and then, in January 2018, to Liverpool.

The Reds paid £75m which, at the time, made Van Dijk both the most expensive defender and the most expensive-ever Dutch player. Van Dijk has repaid the investment many times over.

The partnership with the Anfield club reached a pinnacle with Liverpool's 2019 treble of UEFA Champions League, UEFA Super Cup and FIFA Club World Cup. One year later and Van Dijk helped power Liverpool to their first domestic league crown in 30 years. Hardly surprisingly, he was voted UEFA Men's Player of the Year as well as the Premier League's top player.

Van Dijk's national team career began with the Netherlands' Under-19s and progressed via the Under-21s to a call-up for the senior team in 2014. Not until the following year, however, was Van Dijk eventually able to enjoy a senior debut against Kazakhstan in the EURO qualifiers.

In 2018 Van Dijk was appointed captain by national coach Ronald Koeman, but he had to wait four years before leading the Oranje into a major tournament at the FIFA World Cup finals in Qatar in 2022. They came within a penalty shoot-out of the semi-final before losing out narrowly to Argentina.

RIGHT: Virgil van Dijk was a European club champion with Liverpool in the UEFA Champions League in 2019.

GRANIT XHAKA

Granit Xhaka is one of nine Swiss players honoured with more than a century of appearances for their country during a stellar career which has included an age group world title plus a central role for Switzerland at major international tournaments over the past decade.

Xhaka made his first international mark in 2009 at the FIFA U-17 World Cup, which saw Switzerland beat hosts and holders Nigeria 1-0 in the final. His debut for the senior national team followed two years later.

Xhaka was born and brought up in Basel, one of two international football-playing sons of Kosovo-Albanian parents. Granit decided to play for Switzerland while older brother Taulant opted for Albania. The brothers faced each other on opposite sides at EURO 2016 in Lens with Granit and Switzerland winning 1-0.

Xhaka was already a Swiss regular at the 2014 and 2018 FIFA World Cups as well as at both EURO 2016 and 2020. He celebrated his 100th international in a friendly against Kosovo in March 2022.

Xhaka, at both national team and club level, has earned a rating as one of the most competitive midfielders in European football and been honoured twice as Swiss footballer of the year.

He kicked his first football at Concordia Basel before joining the Basel youth section in January 2003. Within seven years he was making a goalscoring debut in a UEFA Champions League qualifier against Hungary's Debrecen. Two senior seasons brought Swiss league and cup success before Xhaka's transfer to Germany's Borussia Mönchengladbach in 2012.

Xhaka's leadership qualities saw him appointed Borussia club captain before he left for Arsenal in 2016. His seven years in north London included two FA Cup wins before returning to Germany with Bayer Leverkusen in 2022.

RIGHT: Granit Xhaka has been a trophy winner at club level in both Switzerland and England.

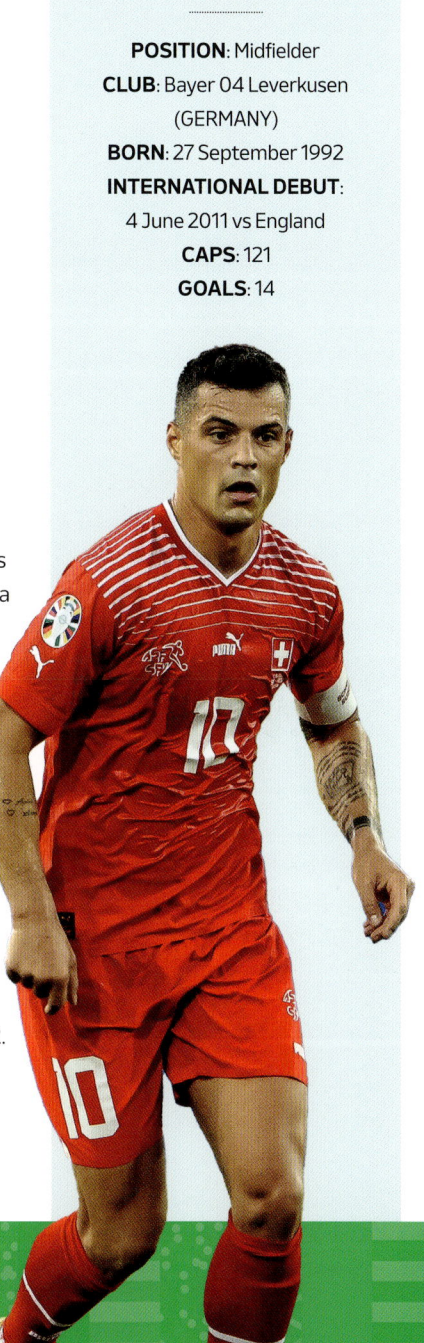

POSITION: Midfielder
CLUB: Bayer 04 Leverkusen (GERMANY)
BORN: 27 September 1992
INTERNATIONAL DEBUT: 4 June 2011 vs England
CAPS: 121
GOALS: 14

2021

Magic Moments:
DEFIANT DONNARUMMA

11 JULY 2021 / WEMBLEY

Italy have twice been crowned champions of Europe and each success has been a triumph of cool nerves. In 1968 the Azzurri beat Yugoslavia in a replay, and at UEFA EURO 2020 they won penalty shoot-outs to beat both Spain in the semi-finals and then hosts England in the Wembley final. Goals from Luke Shaw in the opening minutes and Leonardo Bonucci in the second half left the teams locked at 1-1 after extra time. Italy trailed again by 2-1 in the shoot-out before goalkeeper Gianluigi Donnarumma turned the tables. The 22-year-old's saves from Jadon Sancho and Bukayo Saka edged coach Roberto Mancini's Italy to a 3-2 victory. Donnarumma's three clean sheets, nine saves and concession of only four goals in seven appearances earned him the player of the tournament award from UEFA's panel of technical observers.

RIGHT: Italy's players mob triumphant goalkeeper Gianluigi Donnarumma after he saves England's fifth and last penalty in the UEFA EURO 2020 final at Wembley.

UEFA EURO 2024 PROGRESS CHART

Fill in the match results below as the tournament unfolds. All kick-off times are local and are CEST (Central European Summer Time), which is UTC +2. They are also subject to change.

GROUP A

Date & Time	Home			Away	Venue
14 June, 21:00	Germany	☐	☐	Scotland	Munich
15 June, 15:00	Hungary	☐	☐	Switzerland	Cologne
19 June, 18:00	Germany	☐	☐	Hungary	Stuttgart
19 June, 21:00	Scotland	☐	☐	Switzerland	Cologne
23 June, 21:00	Switzerland	☐	☐	Germany	Frankfurt
23 June, 21:00	Scotland	☐	☐	Hungary	Stuttgart

Team	P	W	D	L	GD	Pts
1						
2						
3						
4						

GROUP B

Date & Time	Home			Away	Venue
15 June, 18:00	Spain	☐	☐	Croatia	Berlin
15 June, 21:00	Italy	☐	☐	Albania	Dortmund
19 June, 15:00	Croatia	☐	☐	Albania	Hamburg
19 June, 21:00	Spain	☐	☐	Italy	Gelsenkirchen
24 June, 21:00	Albania	☐	☐	Spain	Düsseldorf
24 June, 21:00	Croatia	☐	☐	Italy	Leipzig

Team	P	W	D	L	GD	Pts
1						
2						
3						
4						

GROUP C

Date & Time	Home			Away	Venue
16 June, 18:00	Slovenia	☐	☐	Denmark	Stuttgart
16 June, 21:00	Serbia	☐	☐	England	Gelsenkirchen
20 June, 15:00	Slovenia	☐	☐	Serbia	Munich
20 June, 18:00	Denmark	☐	☐	England	Frankfurt
25 June, 21:00	England	☐	☐	Slovenia	Cologne
25 June, 21:00	Denmark	☐	☐	Serbia	Munich

Team	P	W	D	L	GD	Pts
1						
2						
3						
4						

GROUP D

Date & Time	Home			Away	Venue
16 June, 15:00	Play-off A	☐	☐	Netherlands	Hamburg
17 June, 21:00	Austria	☐	☐	France	Düsseldorf
21 June, 18:00	Play-off A	☐	☐	Austria	Berlin
21 June, 21:00	Netherlands	☐	☐	France	Leipzig
25 June, 18:00	Netherlands	☐	☐	Austria	Berlin
25 June, 18:00	France	☐	☐	Play-off A	Dortmund

Team	P	W	D	L	GD	Pts
1						
2						
3						
4						

GROUP E

Date & Time	Home			Away	Venue
17 June, 15:00	Romania	☐	☐	Play-off B	Munich
17 June, 18:00	Belgium	☐	☐	Slovakia	Frankfurt
21 June, 15:00	Slovakia	☐	☐	Play-off B	Düsseldorf
22 June, 21:00	Belgium	☐	☐	Romania	Cologne
26 June, 18:00	Slovakia	☐	☐	Romania	Frankfurt
26 June, 18:00	Play-off B	☐	☐	Belgium	Stuttgart

Team	P	W	D	L	GD	Pts
1						
2						
3						
4						

GROUP F

Date & Time	Home			Away	Venue
18 June, 18:00	Türkiye	☐	☐	Play-off C	Dortmund
18 June, 21:00	Portugal	☐	☐	Czechia	Leipzig
22 June, 15:00	Play-off C	☐	☐	Czechia	Hamburg
22 June, 18:00	Türkiye	☐	☐	Portugal	Dortmund
26 June, 21:00	Play-off C	☐	☐	Portugal	Gelsenkirchen
26 June, 21:00	Czechia	☐	☐	Türkiye	Hamburg

Team	P	W	D	L	GD	Pts
1						
2						
3						
4						

ROUND OF 16

29 June, 21:00, Match 37, Dortmund

Winner Group A v Runner-up Group C

29 June, 18:00, Match 38, Berlin

Runner-up Group A v Runner-up Group B

30 June, 21:00, Match 39, Cologne

Winner Group B v Third place Group A/D/E/F

30 June, 18:00, Match 40, Gelsenkirchen

Winner Group C v Third place Group D/E/F

1 July, 21:00, Match 41, Frankfurt

Winner Group F v Third place Group A/B/C

1 July, 18:00, Match 42, Düsseldorf

Runners-up Group D v Runners-up Group E

2 July, 18:00, Match 43, Munich

Winner Group E v Third place Group A/B/C/D

2 July, 21:00, Match 44, Leipzig

Winner Group D v Runners-up Group F

QUARTER-FINALS

5 July, 18:00, Match 45, Stuttgart

Winner Match 39 v Winner Match 37

5 July, 21:00, Match 46, Hamburg

Winner Match 41 v Winner Match 42

6 July, 21:00, Match 47, Berlin

Winner Match 43 v Winner Match 44

6 July, 18:00, Match 48, Düsseldorf

Winner Match 40 v Winner Match 38

SEMI-FINALS

9 July, 21:00, Match 49, Munich

Winner Match 45 v Winner Match 46

10 July, 21:00, Match 50, Dortmund

Winner Match 47 v Winner Match 48

UEFA EURO 2024 FINAL

14 July, 21:00, Berlin

___ v ___

Goalscorers

Goalscorers

Man of the Match

PICTURE CREDITS

The publishers would like to thank the following sources for their kind permission to reproduce the pictures in this book. (T-top, B-bottom, L-left, R-right)

ALAMY
AP 18-19

COLORSPORT
56-57

GETTY IMAGES
ANP 39; Severin Aichbauer/SEPA.Media 73B; Jose Manuel Alvarez/Quality Sport Images 100R; Anadolu Agency 26B, 100L; Athena Pictures 72B; Mikolaj Barbanell/SOPA Images/LightRocket 102L; Lars Baron 17T, 108; Serhat Cagdas/Anadolu Agency 96L; Jean Catuffe 22B; Matteo Ciambelli/DeFodi Images 109; Emmanuele Ciancaglini/Ciancaphoto Studio 110; Reinaldo Coddou H. 13T; Seb Daly/Sportsfile 74R, 98B; Elianton/Mondadori Portfolio 52R, 53; Stu Forster/Allsport/Hulton Archive 92-93; Foto Olimpik/NurPhoto 24T; Stuart Franklin 14T, 16B; Sebastian Frej/MB Media 25T, 42L, 116, 121; Nigel French/Sportsphoto/Allstar 40R; Jürgen Fromme/firo sportphoto 38L; James Gill/Danehouse 51; Markus Gilliar/GES Sportfoto 38R; Laurence Griffiths 124-125; Georg Hochmuth/APA/AFP 77; Isosport/MB Media 24B; Gilbert Iundt/Corbis/VCG 68-69; Zed Jameson/MB Media 101; Mohammad Karamali/DeFodi Images 118; Attila Kisbenedek/AFP 43; Joe Klamar/AFP 114-115; Jurij Kodrun 25B; Christof Koepsel 15T; Igor Kralj/Pixsell/MB Media 96R; Harry Langer/DeFodi Images 17B, 45, 123; Miroslav Lelas/Pixsell/MB Media 23B; Christian Liewig/Corbis 79; Ross MacDonald/SNS Group 22T; Marcio Machado/Eurasia Sport Images 26T, 44L, 44R; Jure Makovec/AFP 99T; Charles McQuillan 60R; Pedja Milosavljevic/DeFodi Images 65; Dean Mouhtaropoulos 15B; Jonathan Nackstrand/AFP 76L; Nesimages/Michael Bulder/DeFodi Images 119; Alex Nicodim/NurPhoto 91B, 99B; Rene Nijhuis/BSR Agency 75; Ulrik Pedersen/DeFodi Images 63; Ryan Pierse 41; Popperfoto 32-33; Joe Prior/Visionhaus 67; Manuel Queimadelos/Quality Sport Images 49; Carlos Rodrigues 120; Rafal Rusek/PressFocus/MB Media 55; Frederic Scheidemann 11; Alexander Scheuber 13B; Richard Sellers/Sportsphoto/Allstar 23T, 112; Mateusz Slodkowski 103; Igor Soban/Pixsell/MB Media 117; Catherine Steenkeste 78R; Marco Steinbrenner/DeFodi Images 86R; Boris Streubel 111; TF-Images/DeFodi Images 14B; Marcel ter Bals/BSR Agency 122; Bob Thomas Sports Photography 80-81; Joris Verwijst/BSR Agency 84R, 85; James Williamson/AMA 102R; Charlotte Wilson/Offside 40L

SHUTTERSTOCK
xalien 12

UEFA
Reinaldo Coddou H. 6; Stuart Franklin 30-31; Oliver Hardt 98T; Alexander Hassenstein 74L, 84L; Christian Hofer 86L, 87; Richard Juilliart 7; Jurij Kodrun 50L, 50R, 60L, 61; Aurelien Meunier 78L, 113; Alex Morton 10, 104-105; Valerio Pennincino 66L, 66R; Tullio Puglia 52L, 54L, 54R. 62L, 62R, 73T, 76L, 97; Mark Runnacles 48L, 48R; Francesco Scaccianoce 88L, 88R; Srdjan Stevanovic 42R, 64L, 64R; Boris Streubel 72T; Sebastian Widmann 16T

Every effort has been made to acknowledge correctly and contact the source and/or copyright holder of each picture. Any unintentional errors or omissions will be corrected in future editions of this book.